JACK THE
RIPPER

JACK THE RIPPER

100 YEARS OF INVESTIGATION

TERENCE SHARKEY

DORSET PRESS
NEW YORK

First published in Great Britain in 1987 by Ward Lock Ltd.

This edition published by Dorset Press,
a division of Marboro Books Corp.,
by arrangement with Cassel plc

1992 Dorset Press

ISBN 0-88029-729-8

Printed and bound in the United States of America

M 9 8 7 6 5 4 3 2

Contents

Acknowledgments   6
List of victims   7
Preface   8
Introduction   10

1   Whitechapel   13
2   Not so pretty Polly   16
3   Street law   22
4   Dark Annie   25
5   Life, liberty and the pursuit of happy crimes   33
6   Long Liz   37
7   Kate   43
8   Warren's rabbits   50
9   Mary   56
10   Letters from hell   64
11   Person or persons unknown   76
12   Reflections of the Ripper   86
13   Identity parade   91
14   Pick your Ripper   128

Bibliography   142
Index   143

ACKNOWLEDGMENTS

Ripperologists, that band of dedicated sleuths, cannot research far without touching the tracks of certain luminaries in the field. A couple of the most well known are the two Donalds — McCormick and Rumbelow. The knowledge that they have shared with others through their books has been an inspiration and is gratefully acknowledged.

Thanks are also due to Lynn Picknett, for her tireless picture research.

The illustrations, letters and notices reproduced in this book were kindly supplied by the following: the author (page 139); BBC Hulton Picture Library (pages 19, 46, 52, 61 and 81); John Frost (pages 17, 29, 34, 35, 41 and 58); Guildhall Library (page 11); The Public Record Office, ref. MEPO 3 140 (pages 38, 65, 68, 74 and 125); Joseph Sickert (page 105); Topham Picture Library (pages 14, 27, 95, 99 and 130).

AUTHOR'S NOTE

The Decimal Currency Act of 1967, which swept away monetary and measurement titles that had been around for centuries, created problems for authors. Since then, a generation has grown up for whom any reference to shillings or sixpences is as alien as roubles or piastres. The resulting dilemma for the author who wants merely to get on with the storytelling is that bracketed explanations of traditional terms delay the essential action.

Let us have none of this! If Mary Kelly charged half-a-crown for her favours that's what she charged, not $12\frac{1}{2}$ new pence. All values and measurements are given in pre-decimal and imperial terms.

The Victims

POLLY NICHOLS
31 August 1888   Buck's Row, Whitechapel

ANNIE CHAPMAN
8 September 1888   Hanbury Street, Spitalfields

ELIZABETH STRIDE
30 September 1888   Berner Street, Whitechapel

CATHERINE EDDOWES
30 September 1888   Mitre Square, Aldgate

MARY KELLY
9 November 1888   Miller's Court, Dorset Street, Spitalfields

Preface

The twisted and mysterious killer known as Jack the Ripper, a riddle at the peak of his crimes, has become even more of an enigma as time passes. The taunting, boastful butcher of five – some say eleven – women, left few clues. His was one of the most difficult types of murder to solve. Even today the prostitute-victim's necessarily furtive, solitary lifestyle often makes it impossible to track down her killer. The London policeman of 1888 could barely control the destitute thousands of East End inhabitants – a million souls of all types. Muggers, thugs, drunkards, immigrants – legal and illegal – were crowded together in the squalor that lay outside the City walls.

The murder of prostitutes was no remarkable thing in those mean, dark streets, but in the space of three months and with five known victims the silent slayer brought panic, not just to the twelve hundred street walkers, but to the population as a whole. The police were powerless . . .

A century on from these events many think it unlikely that the identity of the Ripper will ever be known. The secret Home Office case-papers, closed since 1892, are gradually being made public. But the haphazard collection in three manilla wrap-around files tied with pink tape offers few clues.

The Macnaghten Papers, the notes written by the then Head of the CID, say little more. These documents and the admission by the chief officer that he had destroyed certain papers in order to protect the family of the major suspect all tend to make the trail of the Ripper a tantalizing but unending pursuit.

The motives attributed to the murderer have been several. Sexual gratification, religious ritual, revenge for disease-contraction, or simply an attempt to clean up the city's seamy streets. But if there are several possible motives, there are scores of theories about the identity of the killer. Most have been based on the belief that the mutilations revealed a skilled hand; a doctor, a midwife, a butcher perhaps. Strong evidential links with the legal profession have been claimed, as was a link with Queen Victoria herself. The latest documents discovered and examined by eminent pathologists have done little to bring us closer to the truth.

This study of the macabre slayings presents no author's prejudice, no convenient bending or omission of the facts but joins the reader in close *active participation* in the investigative process. A unique opportunity to consider personally: why the murders happened; why the victims were chosen; and who it was who stalked the streets of darkness, as well as the chance to test these considerations against known evidence.

The horrifying nature of this greatest of unsolved mysteries calls for strong nerves. For the reader who undertakes the investigation, who follows the trail first to one door and then another, the route is both compelling and fascinating.

East End children still skip to the rhyme:

> Jack the Ripper's dead
> And lying in his bed
> He cut his throat
> With *Sunlight* soap
> Jack the Ripper's dead.

But the rhyme is wrong. True, the monster who dipped his knives into the flesh in Whitechapel has by now joined his victims, away from our world. But the gruesome memory of Jack truly lives on, the fascination of his unsolved crimes ensuring his fleeting figure immortality. Jack the Ripper lives.

Introduction

HER GRAVE IS MARKED with a simple slab. The moss-covered granite shows those who care, whose earthly remains lie here. Mary Jane Kelly's final resting place has a peace and obscurity that her death did not.

Time has not been kind to St Patrick's church. The saintly shield that protected it from the worst of Hitler's bombs has been withdrawn and the hand of nature has taken over. Convolvulus sprouts inquisitive coiling fingers from broken rain-water pipes, ivy clings tenaciously to crumbling brickwork. Enormous monoliths that marked the Victorian graveyard have subsided drunkenly and lilac peeps through the broken slabs of foundations that are no more lasting than the doubtful morality of the age that spawned them.

Around the plot the crumbling monuments stand in silent witness, their legends barely discernible after one hundred years of decay. Mary Kelly's grave would escape the notice of all but the most observant, but for those who seek, it is a reminder: one of five certain facts about a series of crimes that started in the courtyards of teeming tenements and whose vibrations shook at the pillars of the Establishment – and the Royal Family itself.

There are four more of these facts, all established, all certain and all lying similarly interred, dotted around the cemeteries near Whitechapel and its neighbours Leyton and Manor Park. The facts have names and dates and these are certain too. As certain as the one remaining fact – that all shared their solitary calling of prostitution and that all met their death by the slashing knife of a maniacal killer. Beyond these few facts lies the vast blackness of the unknown. The identity of the killer, the motive, even the method have all been called into question.

Occasional flashes of inspiration have pierced the blackness, only to be found wanting in some particular so that the brief illumination dies and renders even blacker the veil of mystery that hangs over these events of the squalid East End streets of Victorian London.

At times the sun's rays pierce the tangled undergrowth and warm the weathered stone, and late on summer evenings the shadow of the angel

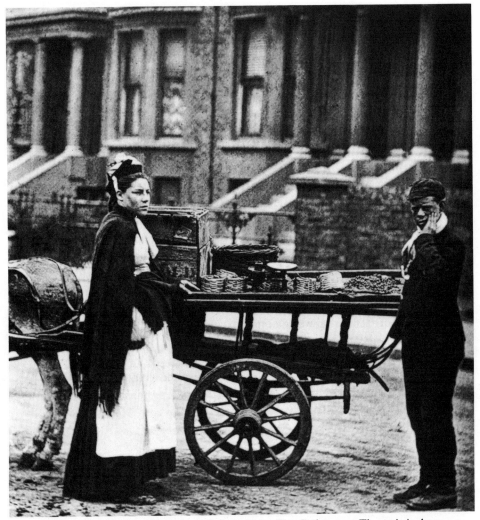

Slum districts were often less than a mile from elegant West End squares. The strain in these faces reflects the times. The servant girl might get £5 a year; a prostitute could earn that in a week, but in Whitechapel that autumn the risks were high.

on a nearby mausoleum falls on Mary's grave. The grand momuments to the Victorian merchants and their wives cast shadows over Mary in death just as their incumbents would have done in life.

The angel wears a puzzled frown as he surveys the nearby East End traffic. He was put here to mark the passing of one William McDonough. His skin was white then, a fine alabaster-marble. A century of London life has left him pock-marked, his whiteness greyed by a hundred winters, complexion flawed by ten thousand sulphurous fogs.

It wasn't always like this. Once street scenes of a different nature had met the angel's gaze. The steady clatter of hooves on cobbles, of iron-ringed cart wheels, of cabbies' whips and costermonger cries. All this before McAdam had stretched his vast tar ribbon across the capital.

It was a different London then. The East End lay outside the City wall. Dank, evil-smelling marshland that was home to nearly two million mortals living below the poverty line in poky one-room hovels. Nightly drunkenness and brawling punctuated the drab existence. Shouts and curses in a babble of tongues reflected the sea of immigrants and refugees that had flooded this part of London from Central and Eastern Europe.

Mary was twenty-five when she was buried in this place. The young Limerick-born Catholic had made her way here via the streets of Cardiff's dockland five years earlier. Raven-haired and attractive, her fresh-complexioned vivacity was uncommon among the majority of the drabs who frequented the dismal taverns. It was said that she had come to London to seek fame and fortune in the smart bordellos of Piccadilly but little is known of her life at that time. What is certain is that by the autumn of 1888 she was pounding the pavements of Whitechapel, available to any man – and some said not only men – who would advance her the price of a drink.

Despite the singularity of her charms, fortune eluded Mary in the bright West End. Only an unenviable fame, permanent and final, awaited her in the shadowy, seamy streets to the east.

1
Whitechapel

THE DISTRICT OF WHITECHAPEL lies in the heart of the East End. It is still not as fashionable as its West End neighbours, but, like other once grimy and sordid boroughs in the area, the Blitz and years of replanning have transformed it. Its more prosperous air has not yet made it the most beautiful part of London, but it is a long way from being the worst slum in the country as it was in Queen Victoria's time. Then, as now, it was home to a polyglot community of immigrants and cockneys whose families had lived there for centuries. Irish migrants, and Polish and Jewish refugees who had fled from the middle-Europe pogroms of the 1860s, lived together in general harmony.

Shabby shops and houses frequented narrow streets that gave access to innumerable stinking courts. These spawned thousands of lodging-houses where for threepence a night a bed in a line of others could be bought. The twentieth-century researcher finds much to astonish: the casual calls on neighbours that people would make at literally all hours of the night; shops open long after midnight; public-houses which, having thrown out their last customer at 3 a.m., would open again to serve liquid breakfast at six. Many of the hovels had no cooking facilities and hot food would be bought from pie shops and the like. A regular sight was the Sunday meat, when there was any, being taken to the bakers to be cooked for twopence.

It was a London less than three miles from the bright lights of Haymarket and Piccadilly, with their 'Mott's Night House' or the notorious 'Kate Hamilton's', where £5 was the admission charge for the wealthy and titled clientele.

The gas and electric lighting that had been in use in the streets 'up West' since the early 1800s had barely reached Whitechapel eighty years later. The shops and better-class houses throughout London had these luxuries, but not the dwellings in the meaner streets, where oil-lamps or candles provided a dismal and sinister illumination.

Street traders were everywhere; costermongers, food-vendors with fried fish, meat pies, pigs' trotters, plum duff, baked potatoes, cat's meat and hot wine. Street showmen of enormous variety proliferated.

Lodgings. 8,500 poor lived a hand to mouth existence in Whitechapel's 233 common lodging-houses, as many as eighty to each fetid dormitory.

Pathetic freaks were exhibited. Albinos, dwarves, elephant-men, pig-faced ladies, performing monkeys, Punch and Judy, black-faced clowns, fortune-telling budgerigars and stilt-walkers. There was street music from the Italianate hurdy-gurdy to the very British one-man-band.

Nearby, the docks area created work for labourers, but it was irregular and depended on the arrival of ships. Men were often employed by the day only. Milliners, dress-makers, furriers, tambour-makers, shoe-binders, pastry cooks, cigar-makers, seamstresses and laundry maids worked long hours and earned little. The vast markets at Spitalfields and Billingsgate supplying meat and fish gave employment, as did the enormous fruit and vegetable market at Covent Garden, but for many there was little chance of honest work, and the teeming rookeries in such places as Clerkenwell, Westminster, the Borough and Whitechapel were their refuge.

Most estates had the typical water-tank, which was turned on for a short time each day, a rat-infested garbage tip that was rarely removed and, serving the whole court, the ever-present, all-pervading lavatory.

The fact that many inhabitants of the East End could remember the last public hanging at Newgate twenty years before did not discourage crime. There were many areas of Whitechapel where the police would only venture in groups, and a mile further east into Dockland's notorious Ratcliffe Highway they would not venture at all. A contemporary writer described it as '. . . a place where crime stalked unmolested, to thread its deadly length was a foolhardy act that might quail the stoutest heart.' Ratcliffe Highway had been the site of a series of brutal and barbaric murders in 1811. Over a period of twelve December nights, two households comprising seven people were clubbed to death. There had been an unprecedented public outcry and a demand for more effective policing. For almost eight decades legends circulated in the East End and the pitiless slaughters were accorded the highest, if unenviable, accolade of the Crime of the Century.

And indeed they were, until one dark night in August 1888, when the gruesome work of a slashing knife made its claim for this grim title.

2

Not so pretty Polly

JOHN PAUL QUICKENED HIS STEP – he had never liked the place. It was familiar enough; he passed this way every day on his way to work, portering at Smithfield market. The homeward walk was different though – it was funny how everything changed in the dark.

Buck's Row narrowed and became darker as he made his way towards Brady Street. Only faint illumination came from the unbroken line of shabby terraced houses. People were getting out of bed to go to work. Others, like dock workers and meat porters from Smithfield, were returning home.

Paul paused for a moment to tie his boot lace, putting his foot against the crumbling low stone wall which guarded the embankment of the East London Railway Company. The line ran under the road and entered the tunnel approach to Whitechapel station. In a couple of hours the station would be busy but now, at 3.15 a.m., it lay silent and shuttered in the darkness. As he straightened up a sudden chill ran down his spine, for on the other side of the street, barely visible against the yellow gaslit interior of one of the dwellings, he could see the figure of a man crouching in the roadway, beside a stable entrance.

As Paul approached, the figure rose in front of him. 'Come and look at this woman', he said, motioning towards a bundle on the ground. A body lying prostrate on the ground was pretty unremarkable in a part of London where drinking dens were six times more numerous than today. Paul looked at the woman and concluded that she was drunk. 'Let's get her on her feet', he said. It was difficult to get hold of the woman in the darkness, and as Paul reached beneath the woman's shoulders he recoiled as a warm stickiness engulfed his hand. As they rolled her over the stranger let out a strangled cry. 'Look! Look at her throat!'

Two sweeping incisions ran the width of the woman's neck and had all but severed the head. The ugly weals cut back to the spinal cord and oozed blood which formed a crimson pool below her head.

Lurid picture journals like the *Illustrated Police News* enjoyed great popularity in Victorian London. Graphic woodcuts informed the less literate, while educated readers relished the blood-chilling text.

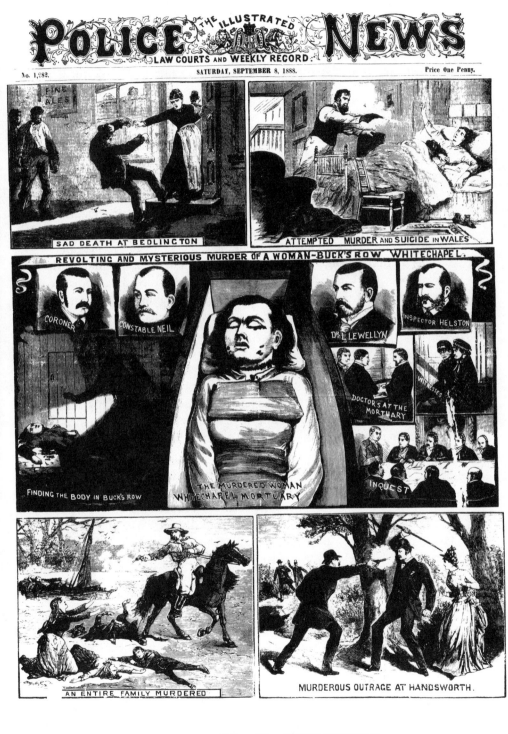

What thoughts went through the two men's minds as each nervously surveyed the other is not recorded. The skirts had been pulled high above the woman's knees, which had led her discoverer to suppose that she had been raped. Now the two men straightened her clothing and, terrified, set off in search of a constable. Three hundred yards further east in Brady Street, where a single street lamp threw fitful but comforting light, they found Police Constable Haine.

Had the two men gone west they would have found the law more quickly, for PC Neil's beat was bringing him towards the scene of the crime, and at the moment Constable Haine was summoned Neil was already shining his lantern on the body of Mary Nichols.

Mary Nichols, or 'Polly' as she was known to her many friends, in the area, was forty-two. Polly had once been pretty – pretty enough to attract printer's machinist William Nichols, marry him and bear five children – but by 1881 her drinking and general slovenliness had resulted in him leaving her. A spell in Lambeth workhouse, a union with a Walworth blacksmith named Drew and a short time as a domestic servant in one of the big merchant's houses on Wandsworth Common were punctuated more and more frequently by bouts of drunkenness. Eventually she became a fugitive from the law, having stolen a measly £3 from her employer.

The last day of August 1888, which was also to be the last day of her life, found Polly as a pathetic drab, old before her time, five front teeth missing and with a history of vagrancy and petty crime. Polly was a female tramp, a prostitute willing to sell herself for the fourpence it would cost to gain re-admittance to the filthy lodgings at 18, Thrawl Street, where she frequently stayed. Earlier that night, penniless, she had been turned away by the lodging-house keeper. Thrawl Street, like its infamous neighbour Flower & Dean Street, had many cheap lodgings for women, but terms were strictly cash-in-advance.

Though only 5 ft 2 in tall, Polly was tough. 'I'll be back. Look what a fine bonnet I've got', she told the lodging-house keeper. Was she going to pawn it? Unlikely, as it was so late, and in any case the item would have fetched little. Could she possibly have thought that the black straw bonnet, velvet-trimmed though it might be, would have guaranteed her doubtful charms?

The last person to have claimed to have seen Polly alive was a friend, Emily Holland, who had spoken to her around 2.30 a.m. at the corner of

Buck's Row – now Durward Street. The discovery of the body near a kosher slaughterhouse started a wave of anti-semitism.

Whitechapel Road and Osborne Street. They often used the same doss-house. Although a pathetic character, there was something about Polly – perhaps her infectious sense of humour or her very gaiety in the face of problems and geniality even in drink. Whatever the quality, it was missing tonight, and Emily was concerned about her. Tonight Polly was so drunk she could scarcely stand. But she would not heed her friend's advice to stay with her, and instead, reeled off down Osborne Street.

The next time Emily saw her, the bonnet was gone, the brown ulster, the brown linsey frock, petticoats, stays and black wool stockings were gone – and her friend was gone. The mortal remains of Polly Nichols were identified by Emily Holland in the mortuary attached to the Old Montague Street workhouse.

Doctor Llewellyn, who lived near Buck's Row, had performed an initial and very perfunctory examination of the body in the gutter at Buck's Row. Even allowing for the fact that it was carried out in the light of four police bull's-eye lanterns, under the steady gaze of a crowd of onlookers, it seems remarkable that the doctor failed to notice that Polly had been disembowelled. Her stomach had been hacked open and slashed many times. Several incisions ran across the abdomen, which had been repeatedly slashed and cut, and the killer had used a knife, possibly with a six to eight inch blade, on her vagina.

Polly's husband had not seen her for three years and there had been little to endear her to him, but one look at the mutilations moved him to murmur 'I forgive you for everything, now that I have seen you like this'.

The newspapers of the day reported events in much more detail than their modern counterparts, and the violence and frenzy of the attack can readily be seen from this account in the *Star*:

> No murder was ever more ferociously and brutally done. The knife, which must have been a large and sharp one, was jabbed into the deceased at the lower part of the abdomen and then drawn upwards not once but twice. The first cut veered to the right, slitting up the groin and passing over the left hip, but the second cut went straight upward along the centre of the body, and reaching to the breast-bone. Such horrible work could only be the work of a maniac.

Later victims bore similar injuries – upward forceful thrusts, the unmistakable autograph of one assailant.

The elementary blunder on the part of the doctor in failing to notice that the victim had been butchered, ripped from belly to throat, and the subsequent premature removal of the body by the police may have destroyed vital clues. The carelessness or even culpable negligence at the scene of the crime was compounded by the fact that Whitechapel had no public mortuary and the body was taken to the workhouse mortuary, where it was dealt with not by a professional but merely a pauper inmate. Robert Munn had stripped and washed the body before the post-mortem could be carried out.

When later the question 'Why so little blood at the scene?' was posed it could not be answered. It was unlikely that the body had been transported there. Front doors opened almost directly into the street. A carriage would have been heard and noticed. Anyway, how much blood had there been? Nobody knew. The police had washed it away as soon as the body had been removed.

Jack certainly had luck on his side. People had been sleeping, and indeed were lying awake, within feet of where the body, still warm, was found. Police patrols passed the spot every thirty minutes. With three watchmen, four policeman and more able to converge on the body in under a minute, and early-morning workers moving around, how had the killer managed his task so silently and his escape, with bloody hands and clothes, so completely? It was early days. Whitechapel had seen nothing yet.

3

Street Law

'Y OU AIN'T GOT NO RIGHT, I'm a good girl I am.' Lisa was angry and frightened, the constable's grip was tight on her arm. She remembered what some of the older girls had told her. 'You see what 'appens when I talk to your sergeant. It's not fair, you ain't got no right at all.'

She was wrong of course. 'They' had always had rights. Rights to arrest prostitutes, their pimps and brothel-keepers had been enshrined in law as long ago as 1161, with Henry II's enactments insisting that brothel-keepers be free of the pox. Later monarchs had strengthened these laws, which were designed to protect the harlot as well as her client, and other laws set down maximum payment for lodging and provided imprisonment for anyone detaining a woman against her will.

The law that gave PC William Smith of H Division the right to take young Lisa down to Leman Street police station had been around a long time and is still largely the code by which the street-walker is arrested today. The nineteenth-century backlash against the permissive society resulted in the public nuisance laws which encouraged prosecutions against bawdy-houses.

Lisa would spend the night in the cell at Leman Street police station with the other girls, and having had time to think it over would plead guilty. With a first offence she might get off with a warning, otherwise it was forty shillings, and that took some finding. Poor Lisa – whilst trying to supplement her meagre earnings as a seamstress she had fallen foul of the Metropolitan Police Act of 1839, which had made it an offence to loiter. Although this Act originally applied only to London, other large towns quickly followed suit, and by the middle of the century the pavement-pounders had been driven into the public-houses.

Lisa was right about one thing though: it wasn't fair. Even among unfortunates there was class distinction. The Vagrancy Act of 1824 had cunningly made vagrants of common prostitutes, thus catching the street-walkers but not assailing the liberty of their courtesan sisters, who operated from safe premises.

Publicans were punished if they 'allowed common prostitutes to assemble and continue' on their premises. The relatively enlightened legislators of 1888 had by the recent Criminal Law Amendment Act raised the age of consent to thirteen. Procurers of girls below that age could be punished with penal servitude for life. Even at fifteen, anyone harbouring Lisa could get two years, so the pubs offered no shelter to her and her pathetic kind, who were really little more than children. It was from shop doorways that Lisa and thousands like her would ask of likely-looking strangers 'Looking for a friend, sir?', and eventually come to accept the inevitable court appearance as part of the price of the game of survival.

The busy law-makers had also been addressing themselves to the problems of sexually transmitted disease. Fifteenth-century laws denied entry to brothels to any male suffering from VD. The Victorians, beset by a 'pestilence of grand proportion' took steps to contain the outbreak. Venereal disease, considered to be a major scourge amongst street-walkers, was found by social reformer Henry Mayhew not to be as grave a problem as many thought:

> One of the peculiarities of this class (Haymarket street-walker) is their remarkable freedom from disease. Syphilis is rarely fatal. It is an entirely distinct race that suffers from the ravages of the insidious diseases that the licence given to the passions and promiscuous intercourse engender. Young girls, innocent and inexperienced, whose devotion has not yet bereft them of their innate modesty and sense of shame will allow their systems to be so shocked and their constitutions so impaired, before the aid of the surgeon is sought for, that when he does arrive his assistance is almost useless.

That the Chief Army Medical Officer clearly did not share Mayhew's generally optimistic note can be seen in an Act of Parliament still in force today. The Contagious Diseases Act of 1864 made medical examination of the prostitute compulsory. Those suffering from VD were incarcerated. At the time of the Whitechapel murders one soldier in four was affected and in India, the jewel of the Empire, British militarism was not the only thing that Tommy Atkins spread. Every other soldier there had the pox. Of course there were those who protested that compulsory medical checks were an infringement of civil liberty, but still the Act was enforced, continuing unbroken up to present times in the FFI (Free From Infection) inspections in the armed services.

The authorities have not always been crushingly oppressive of the prostitute, as illustrated in the public-spirited notion mooted by

Scotland Yard's Vice Squad in February 1987. The Yard was still smarting from an unsuccessful and expensive attempt to prosecute a south London woman, Cynthia Payne. Affectionately dubbed by the press 'Madame Sin', she had allegedly kept a disorderly house in a quiet residential street in Streatham. To overcome this problem, the Yard suggested, why not have legal brothels run by London boroughs? What the men from the Yard apparently did not realize was that the idea was not new. Six hundred years ago no less a body than the Corporation of the City of London was running legalized brothels, its aldermen, as official pimps, discovering that the streets of London were indeed paved, if not with gold, at any rate with quite rich pickings.

In the event, the Yard's suggestion was not followed up. The comings and goings of young – and not so young – men, entertained by nurses and French maids, was left safely to private enterprise, and the overworked Directors of Parks and Recreation in many a London town hall breathed a sigh of relief!

4

Dark Annie

BARELY A WEEK WAS TO PASS before the ghastly autograph would be signed again. In that time the police, finding no apparent motive for the murder of Polly Nichols, nor for two previous prostitute murders that year, those of Emma Smith (3 April) and Martha Tabram (7 August), concluded that the motive was an intense hatred of prostitutes. Men who had aired such thoughts publicly were sought and a number of suspects were questioned. Soon the newspapers were proclaiming the arrest of a Whitechapel boot-maker, John Pizer, who was known to beat up whores when he was drunk. However, the knives found at his lodgings were easily explained away by his trade. On top of this his alibi was strong, so he was released. His was the nickname 'Leather Apron' that was to figure so prominently in police enquiries.

Although it is now generally accepted that Nichols was the first actual Ripper victim, it is not difficult to appreciate the concern that had been mounting for some time previously in the East End. There had been three murders in five months. Admittedly, Emma Smith claimed she had been attacked by four men but the public had heard about the dreadful internal injuries that had been inflicted and these were superseded in the case of Tabram, who was found with no less than thirty-nine puncture wounds in her body.

Polly Nichols, they thought, had been killed by the same frenzied hand, but later investigations showed clear dissimilarities between the murders. In the case of Smith, her assailants were believed to be members of the notorious Old Nichol Gang. The Bethnal Green street from which they got their name had been a centre of East End crime for more than a century. The gang used methods as varied as terrorizing prostitutes and sending children out to shoplift. Dickens has told it all.

Things were particularly bad at the end of summer, 1888. The people of the East End were close to panic; local traders were losing business as people from neighbouring districts shunned Whitechapel, and the area was beginning to get an even more unsavoury reputation than hitherto. A sickening pattern was emerging – a sadistic maniac was at large and the police were powerless.

Hanbury Street runs eastwards from London's major meat market, Spitalfields, to Whitechapel, passing through an area that was in the last century one of the most feared districts in the East End. It was a street of dingy, three-storied houses, with shops on the ground floor and flats above them. On the top floor of number twenty-nine there lived John Davis, an elderly porter from Spitalfields, with his wife. Fourteen other tenants crammed into the tiny dwelling. At that time the shop beneath was a barber's. Beside the shop a passage ran through the building, with a door at each end. The passage led to an untidy backyard, a patchwork of stones and earth.

The beginning of the weekend was a busy time at the meat market. In those days before the refrigerator the Sunday joint would be purchased on Saturday, and Davis was up early to perform this task. At six o'clock, about to leave for work, he went out into the yard. A meat porter is not generally squeamish about blood, he lives daily with the sight and smell of it, but even John Davis was not prepared for the image that smashed into his senses as he swung back the door from the house.

Beside the two stone steps down into the yard, between them and the fence of number twenty-seven, was the mangled body of a woman. She lay discarded in the familiar rape position, on her back, knees drawn up and outwards, feet resting on the ground. Her hands were raised with the palms outwards, her left arm across her left breast. Her face was clearly visible. Her dirty black skirt had been pulled above her knees. Her entrails were strewn around her body.

Davis ran screaming into the street where he gasped out the details of his find to two passing workmen. In the market-place they found a policeman, who remarkably declined to come with them on the grounds that the murder had not taken place on his beat. Back in Hanbury Street the men's cries of 'Murder!' were heard by Detective Inspector Joseph Chandler, a more peripatetic officer than his subordinate. A crowd had gathered and the detective had some difficulty forcing his way through the passage. Mercifully the remains had now been covered with a tarpaulin. After arranging for telegrams to be sent to various officers, including Detective Inspector Abberline of Scotland Yard, who had assisted at the Nichols murder enquiry, Chandler set about looking for clues.

By the time the Divisional Surgeon, Dr George Bagster-Phillips arrived some minutes later, the houses surrounding the yard were crowded with sightseers. Apparently some were even charged a small fee for access to the windows! The murderer had made sure that their ghoulish curiosity would not go unrewarded. Indeed for some onlookers

29, Hanbury Street. The killer reached the garden through the passage door on the left of the picture. Typical of many cheap lodging-houses, sixteen people lived there and the front and back doors were left open, coincidentally providing a rendezvous for prostitutes and their clients.

the sights were more than they had bargained for, and several flat-dwellers, having sold grandstand tickets, later found themselves with unenviable cleaning-up tasks.

Dr Bagster-Phillips rolled back the tarpaulin to reveal the body, clothed in a long black coat and skirt, over red and white bloodstained stockings. His nimble fingers untied the handkerchief around the neck, but he was unprepared for the result: as he fumbled with the knot the head rolled sideways, attached to the body by only a thin strip of skin. The doctor took his grim inventory. Above the dead woman's right shoulder were a piece of her abdomen and her small intestine, attached by a cord that ran back to the rest of the intestines inside the body. Closer examination revealed more flaps of skin from the abdomen at the left shoulder, soaked in a pool of blood.

The tableau was made more ghastly by the curious placing of objects apparently taken from the victim. At the feet were two brass rings and two bright new farthings. At the head there were two pills wrapped in a screw of paper and a piece of an envelope marked with the seal of the Sussex Regiment. Phillips turned over the scrap of paper and beside the letters 'M' and 'sp' he found a post office date stamp reading 'London 28 Aug 1888'.

The final curiosity and one which, like the other items, led the police to many fruitless enquiries, lay under a water tap which projected from the fence about three feet from the body. Screwed up and soaking beneath the tap was a leather apron.

Later that afternoon the doctor attended the mortuary to examine the body more closely, but he was hampered by the fact that it had been washed and stripped, only the handkerchief having been left in place to prevent the head separating from the torso.

Timothy Donovan, a lodging-house keeper identified the body as that of Annie Chapman, known locally as 'Dark Annie'. He kept the lodgings at 35, Dorset Street and she had been seen in the kitchen there at two o'clock that morning. Donovan had turned Annie out when she had been unable to pay for her bed. Ironically, it may be that from the piteous coins beside her body she may in fact have had the few pennies required to give her the safety of the lodgings.

Although a longstanding prostitute well-known in the Stratford area of east London, Annie had seen better times. She had been married to a

Speculation was fuelled by gratuitous references to slaughtermen in this *Illustrated Police News* front page spread. The paper warned readers to look out for a killer transformed into a maniac by epileptic seizure.

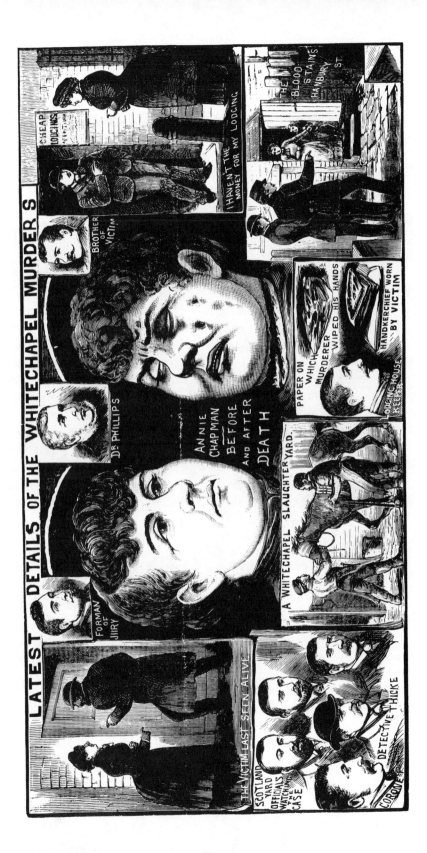

veterinarian who was an army pensioner. To assist with his pension Mr Chapman had latterly worked as a coachman. There had been two children, a deformed son in a cripples home and a daughter who was in an institution in France. Annie had lived in Windsor until she had left her husband about four years before, probably because of her fondness for gin. His allowance of ten shillings a week to her had ceased on his death in 1886.

Dark Annie, with her blue eyes and wavy brown hair, was plump, well-proportioned and forty-seven years old. She looked several years older, and with the loss of her front teeth – probably in one of her frequent brawls – she presented no attractive sight. Nevertheless, Donovan was quite sure that she frequently entertained men at Dorset Street.

The inquest took place on 10 September before Mr Wynne E. Baxter at the Working Lads Institute in Whitechapel Road, where, several days before, the hearing on Polly Nichols had found 'wilful murder against person or persons unknown'. The meeting room on the second floor was packed to overflowing and was hot and stuffy. It was hardly surprising that in such an atmosphere, and with the revelation of such harrowing details a number of spectators both male and female passed out.

It may have been these distractions that caused the coroner to clear the court for the most horrific parts of Doctor Bagster-Phillips' evidence. Next day *The Times* described these further details as unfit for publication. With its more restricted readership the *Lancet* had no such qualms:

> The abdomen had been entirely laid open; the intestines, severed from their mesenteric attachments, had been lifted out of the body, and placed on the shoulder of the corpse; whilst from the pelvis, the uterus and its appendages, with the upper portion of the vagina and the posterior two-thirds of the bladder, had been entirely removed. No trace of these parts could be found.

In answer to the coroner, Dr Bagster-Phillips said the minimum time an expert would take to perform such a task would be fifteen minutes. He considered the surgery skilled. Noting that the womb had been removed the Coroner concluded that 'both Nichols and Chapman had been murdered for some object, to secure some pathological specimen from the abdomen'. With these eighteen words a hornet's nest was overturned. The appalling motive was published widely and the talk of resurrectionists sent a chill through Whitechapel, reviving memories of Burke and Hare, Edinburgh bodysnatchers who had been caught and executed sixty years before. A representative of a medical school told of being approached by a wealthy American who wished to issue specimen organs with a book that he was writing. Scotland Yard was informed, but nothing further was heard.

A steady procession of witnesses affirmed Annie's lifestyle. Later Mrs Richardson described the polyglot occupants of her house: in the back room lived an old woman, Sarah Cox; Mr and Mrs Copsey, cigar-makers, lived in the second-floor back; a carman, Mr Thompson, his wife and adopted daughter occupied the front room; in the room on the first floor overlooking the yard lived Alfred Walker and his father. The front parlour in this menagerie was used as a cat's meat shop, in which a Mrs Hardman not only conducted her business but had the dubious pleasure of sleeping as well. Her son also slept in the room. The landlady and her son lived on the ground floor.

All these people had crossed and re-crossed the yard at various times throughout the night. The landlady's son admitted that local prostitutes sometimes took clients into the yard behind the house, and that he visited the yard frequently in order to discourage them. His was the leather apron, which he had left out to dry the night before it was apparently used by the killer in his post-mortem ablutions.

The dead woman had been seen haggling with a man outside number twenty-nine at 5.30 a.m. By 6 a.m. she was dead, and the mutilations would have taken fifteen minutes. A number of witnesses gave descriptions of men seen with Annie. So many witnesses. So many men.

The score was now four unsolved murders in five months and the local traders were getting desperate. The following notice was published:

> Finding that, in spite of murders being committed in our midst our police force is inadequate to discover the author or authors of the late atrocities, we the undersigned have formed ourselves into a committee and intend offering a substantial reward to anyone, citizen or otherwise, who shall give such information as will be the means of bringing the murderer or murderers to justice.

Would money compensate for what was claimed to be bungling inefficiency that had followed in the wake of each crime? The police certainly were not short of suggestions. Letters from all over the nation began to arrive at Scotland Yard. The amateur sleuths were out in force.

But when a Member of Parliament, Samuel Montague, offered the immense sum of £500 reward, the stream of letters became a torrent.

Murder of Annie Chapman: description of main suspects

Description of a man who entered a passage of a house where the murder was committed of a prostitute at 2 a.m. on 8 September. Age thirty-seven. Height 5 ft 7 in. Rather dark beard and moustache; dress – dark jacket, dark vest and trousers, black scarf and black felt hat, spoke with foreign accent.

This notice, put out by Inspector Abberline, was vague and served no useful purpose other than to convey the impression that the police were taking action. It is curious that this description of a solitary man should have been circulated in preference to that of the man seen by two women at 5.30 a.m., haggling with (almost certainly) the victim. A park-keeper's wife and another woman described the man thus: 'Man was dark, shabby-genteel appearance, deerstalker hat (probably brown).'

5

Life, Liberty and the Pursuit of Happy Crimes

THE SMALL SHOPS AND TAVERNS of Whitechapel rang with the babble of many languages as conjecture was piled upon conjecture. The inhabitants of the East End spent uncomfortable nights wondering when the fiend would strike again.

Were it not for the more recent example of cockney courage, fortitude and wit during the wartime blitz, it might be difficult to imagine that, despite the terrors by night, day-time life continued pretty much as normal. Although the newspapers of the time reflected an all-pervasive fear of the killer, many of the reports show that Jack's presence had a lighter side and had become part of grim street-humour.

Young men, said to be medical students, would lurk around White-chapel in the shortening evenings and jump out on unsuspecting passers-by, crying out that the Ripper had come. A report in the *Illustrated Police News* the week after the final murder notes one Pulteney Garrett, a twenty-year-old medical student, who was impri-soned following a disturbance at Mansion House during the Lord Mayor's Show. Pulteney admitted that he had jumped playfully on a policeman's back. He complained of excessive force in being taken to the police station, which he reached in an almost insensible condition, his tongue hanging out and gasping for breath. It was claimed that he had bitten a policeman's knuckles and the officer produced his tooth-marked fist in evidence.

One can't help feeling that the student really was unfortunate in having to face this particular magistrate judging disorders at the Lord Mayor's Show, for on the bench was Mr Alderman Whitehead, the new Lord Mayor himself. The student was fined £5 or a month's hard labour. The Alderman clearly had his own ideas as to how the constable's fist had come into contact with Pulteney's teeth and rejected that evidence as inconclusive.

Among Pulteney's cronies there had been shouts of 'Look out, here's Leather Apron!' Clearly even at the annual festivities, thoughts of the maniacal killer were not far from the public mind.

One particularly startling prankster is reported as having dressed-up

POLICE

THE ILL

LAW COURTS AND V

No. 1,284.　　　　　　　　　　　　　　　　SATURDAY,

Slaughterers, leather-workers, foreigners, body snatchers. Every week the illustrated 'dreadfuls' were filled with both fresh conjecture and suggestions for the reader's protection.

as a skeleton, his face completely white with coal-black sunken eyes, whose merriment consisted of leaping out of the evening darkness into the path of passing-women, crying 'Meet Jack!' The effect on the ladies is best left to the imagination. Following complaints to their menfolk, the joker's body, still in costume and make-up, was found floating in the Thames.

Several individuals claiming to be Leather Apron gave themselves up to police during the enquiries. All were either drunk or found to be harmless lunatics. None was detained.

Despite the hysteria, Londoners' thirst after curious spectacle was not quenched, and many were still willing to be out on the streets late in the evening. For sixpence they could see at the Royal Aquarium Monsieur Blondin celebrating sixty years on the high wire. At the American Museum, York Street, Westminster, a 'Colossal Picture of the Great Falls at Niagara' was promised, with original effects and lit by electric light. Jules Gautier, French champion swimmer, swam $3\frac{1}{2}$ miles from Westminster Bridge to London Bridge with his hands and feet tied together.

The intrepid parachutist Professor Baldwin dropped six thousand

READY FOR THE WHITECHAPEL FIEND. WOMEN SECRETLY ARMED.

feet through the skies of north London, from a balloon. The event had been widely advertised for many weeks and thousands had journeyed by road and rail to Alexandra Palace. Unfortunately the professor's journey did not finish in the same place: the wind blew him into Highgate Woods where his descent ended in the trees. Luckily, he was not injured.

Under the headline 'Jack the Ripper for the night' the *Star* told the story of a youth of nineteen who, after knocking down two women, informed the police that he was Jack for one night only. This Jack was kept off the streets with two months hard labour.

The *Illustrated Police News*, always eager to take up the pen to report crimes of violence, reported that Rippermania had reached Glasgow, where following an attack on a thirty-year-old woman in St Vincent Street, police were looking for a sailor-like man with dark whiskers. The instructions issued to the constables by their dour Scottish superiors were unequivocal:

> The Whitechapel tragedies are causing the Glasgow police to take extra precautions. All the policemen have per circular, been instructed to keep their ears open and if they hear any cry of distress such as 'help' 'murder' or 'police' they are to hasten to the spot at once.

What the constables usually did on hearing such cries is not recorded.

The practice of newspaper-sellers yelling out lurid headlines stopped sometime after the Second World War and perhaps the home-going crowds in large cities have lost something by this. I remember as a child in the 1950s the hurried arrival of another special edition of the evening papers being trumpeted, as the full horror of events in Reg Christie's little house in Notting Hill Gate was revealed. 'Fifth body found – read all abaht it – *Star, Noos, Standard*. Police diggin' up the garden. Police tearin' down the walls.' Whatever the mild, apparently otherwise inoffensive, mass killer did for circulation of the London evening papers in that Coronation year paled into insignificance besides the efforts of Jack. The newspapers were having a field day. By November of 1888 at least one *Daily Telegraph* reader was heartily sick of the cacophony in the streets:

> Sir, can nothing be done to prevent a set of hoarse ruffians coming nightly about our suburban squares and streets yelling at the tops of their hideous voices: 'Special edition – Whitechapel murder– another of 'em – mutilation – special edition – beautiful, awful murder!' And so on, and nearly frightening the life out of the sensitive women and children of the neighbourhood?

In Marylebone police took into custody a man of thirty-six and charged him with being drunk and disorderly. He'd been standing in Marylebone Road shouting at an increasingly angry crowd 'I am Leather Apron, I'll do you like the Whitechapel victims.' When he awoke the next morning sober, Henry Bates probably counted himself very lucky to be in one piece despite the consideration of ten shillings, or seven days, that was the price of his monologue. Sending another man to prison for fourteen days the Clerkenwell magistrate warned that he would send to jail, without option of fine, every man subsequently brought before him for shouting that he was the Whitechapel murderer.

At the height of the killings the following report appeared in the *Star*:

> A man dressed in women's clothing was arrested on suspicion in Goswell Street on Saturday night. He proved he could have nothing to do with the murder, and said he put female attire on only 'for a lark' but he will be brought before the magistrate charged with having done it for an immoral purpose.

Poor H Division, with many of the detectives themselves disguised as women, perhaps even the arresting officer, it is small wonder that the newspapers found much levity in their reports of the authorities' efforts. But these were only an interlude.

6

Long Liz

The rain was falling sluggishly on the cobbles of Berner Street, everything felt cold and clammy to the touch. The distant moan of a steam tug was echoed by the great clock of Christ Church, Spitalfields, calling the four quarters and pausing dolefully before throwing itself into the single hour. Under the arches of the London and Blackwall Railway Company a solitary gas lamp cast its sickly yellow glare over the worn uneven stones, glinting on the iron-rimmed wheels of the little trap as it lurched and clattered in uneven noisy progress along the sodden street.

Tonight seemed wrapped in a muffler of damp haze and the hooves of the little pony threw up spatters of mud which clung for a moment to the oil-skinned driver, before sliding down in the rivulets that fell around his feet. At the end of Berner Street the two-wheeler slowed to enter a dark courtyard. A pair of large wooden gates, wide open, pressed themselves against the tall, long, windowless walls that flanked either side of the entrance, forming a passage of total darkness some twenty feet long and about nine feet wide.

The passage gave way to a small courtyard that was bounded on the right by the wall of a working-men's club occupying the whole length of the court. Lights were on and the windows contrasted with the darkness on the opposite side where the tailors and cigarette-makers who occupied the cottages had turned in for the night. The lights from the club fell on the cottages, intensifying the gloom in the court.

Despite the darkness, the pony was sure-footed as he trod the familiar stones, his feet clattering on the irregular boulders that ran down the centre of the passage. The crouching oil-skinned figure released the reins in anticipation of the end of his journey. Suddenly, in terror, the animal shied to the left, almost throwing the driver from the trap's box seat. The driver cursed and tapped the creature with the whip but, terrified, it would not move, pressing itself further against the left-hand wall, sensing some unknown peril in the inky blackness. The driver, perhaps also conscious of danger, reached over and prodded the blackness with his whip. The leather tip met something – large and

POLICE NOTICE.

TO THE OCCUPIER.

On the mornings of Friday, 31st August, Saturday 8th, and Sunday, 30th September, 1888, Women were murdered in or near Whitechapel, supposed by some one residing in the immediate neighbourhood. Should you know of any person to whom suspicion is attached, you are earnestly requested to communicate at once with the nearest Police Station.

Metropolitan Police Office,
30th September, 1888.

soft – which the pony was determined not to pass. The flickering light of a match revealed to the driver what with keener senses the terrified animal had already discovered. Now the terror was shared.

The International Working Men's Educational Club was considered by many of its neighbours to be nothing more than a noisy drinking club, where Saturday nights would culminate in noisy singing and revelry. In fact the serious aims of the Socialist League that had started the club were largely realized, in both its membership and activities. It drew its followers mainly from the many Russians, Poles and continental Jews who made up the diverse East End community, but any working man who professed Socialism was welcomed, whatever his nationality.

That evening there had been a meeting at 8.00 p.m. on the necessity of Socialism among Jews and more than a hundred had attended. By eleven o'clock most had gone, leaving thirty or so members to begin a laughing, impromptu concert whose noise spilled out into the dark courtyard.

The singing stopped raggedly as a gesticulating, dripping figure appeared in the doorway. In a moment the crowd was outside, bearing candles to illuminate the scene. It was a ghastly picture. A hideous pool of blood in the courtyard outside the door had run from the alley, tracing its ruby pattern in the crevices and pausing to dam into little pools between the round irregular stones, each spawning little streams that trickled off in new directions. Almost half a gallon of the gore had spread itself in this way and the now silent crowd stood incredulous and impotent. No one knew who set up the cry for the police, but it galvanized the onlookers, who set off to scour the nearby streets.

The bull's-eye lamp of Police Constable William Smith disclosed the still-warm body of a middle-aged woman, clothed in a black velvet, feather-trimmed jacket. Her black dress was hitched up revealing white stockings and dark boots. The red rose at her breast was crumpled and streaked with crimson and her bloodstained fingers were locked around a packet of cachous. The outfit was completed by a wide silk scarf, but not wide enough to hide the gaping wound, bearing witness to the one savage slash that had cut the throat from ear to ear, right back to the spine.

It was almost two weeks before the body was positively identified. The inquest at the Vestry Hall in nearby Cable Street heard that the victim was Elizabeth Stride, known as 'Long Liz', who had lived in the district for almost twenty years since arriving from her native Sweden. The register at the Swedish church in Trinity Square showed her maiden name as Gustaafsdotter, and she had been born at Gothenburg on 27 November 1843. A rough entry in the ledger showed that some time after her arrival, probably in 1869, she was said to have married John Thomas Stride. Of Mr Stride there was no sign, perhaps because, as Liz had claimed, he had drowned in the wreck of the *Princess Alice*.

Memories of the Thames disaster when the *Bywell Castle* steam collier had run down the crowded pleasure steamer were still fresh, although it had happened a full ten years before. Tripock Point, Woolwich Arsenal, was less than six miles away; almost six hundred had died there and many had been local people. But if Liz Stride's tragic story of the loss of her ship's carpenter husband and two of their nine children had been given little credence in life, the spotlight of the coroner's inquiry left few doubts that the legend was some pathetic tale dreamed up by Liz, perhaps to justify her descent to the streets of Whitechapel where she plied her trade.

At Woolwich Town Hall the list of victims aboard the *Princess Alice* showed no Stride. Whole families had been drowned but only one instance recorded a father and two children, and they were named Bell. A few bodies had been cast ashore on the other side of the river in Essex and had been dealt with by that county's coroner. Some bodies would have been washed out to sea and would not have appeared in the accounts, but another list existed. The Lord Mayor had been moved to start a fund for dependents and it could reasonably be expected that Liz Stride would not have been too proud to have claimed if she had really sustained the loss. There is no entry in the Mansion House records.

At the inquest a collection of men came forward to state that they had lived with Liz Stride at various times, and Dr Blackwell, whom the police had called to Berner Street, stated quite emphatically that judging from her appearance she belonged to an immoral class. The pastor from the Swedish church who had identified her body gallantly suggested that she made her living from a little sewing. Despite this, as the inquest progressed it became clear that the maniacal killer had not deviated in his choice of victim.

The crime bore one striking dissimilarity from the previous horrors: this time there was no other injury. It was thought that the killer had simply grasped his victim's silk scarf and abruptly pulled her backwards. The windpipe had been severed swiftly allowing her no opportunity to cry out, and almost all her lifeblood had drained away, but there had been no other knife mark. No frenzied slashing of flesh, no careful collage of innards around the corpse. If the killer had intended further injury he had clearly been interrupted.

Lewis Diemshitz, who had discovered the body when returning from work, told the court that in addition to his cheap jewelry trade he and his wife assisted in the management of the mens' club. Something of a master of understatement, Diemshitz is quoted as saying of his concern for his wife at the scene of the carnage; 'I ran indoors to find my wife, she has a weak constitution and anything of that kind shocks her.'

A field day for the Press. In mid October, the double murder vied with the headless torso found during excavations for the new Metropolitan Police headquarters at Scotland Yard.

Several of the jovial choristers from the club said that they had visited the yard. The front door was locked and returning members had to come back in the same way that Diemshitz and the pony had entered. It was certain that the body had not been there twenty minutes before. A curious anomaly developed when Diemshitz insisted that he had seen a bunch of grapes clutched in the dead woman's hand. The coroner reminded him that only the pack of breath-sweetening lozenges had been found at the post-mortem.

One of the witnesses was Dr Barnardo, the social reformer and founder of the children's homes, who had met Liz in the kitchen of a doss-house at 32, Flower & Dean Street. She had seemed depressed and was the worse for drink.

Around the area of Whitechapel there were many warehouses belonging to the dye trade, and it was in one of these that a key witness named William Marshall worked as a labourer. He had seen Long Liz just before midnight, kissing and cuddling a well-dressed middle-aged man, short and stout with a small, round, peaked cap, sailor style. He had heard plainly the mild, well-educated voice saying, 'You'd say anything but your prayers', and Liz laughing gaily at it. She had also been seen with the man at 12.30 a.m. by PC Smith and fifteen minutes later by a late supper-seeker on his way to a chandler's on the corner of Berner Street; he had heard her say, 'Not tonight, some other night'. A quarter of an hour later her body was found.

Within fifteen minutes Liz Stride had moved silently and swiftly from the obscurity of the ill-lit East End streets to national and lasting fame. Jack the Ripper, though clearly interrupted, had struck again.

7

Kate

THE SLEAZY STREETS OF THE East End bear names that seem to have been selected by their builders with some contrariness; stinking alleys have grandiose titles and moth-eaten, scarcely verdant spaces are glorified with the name 'park'. For the visitor in 1888 any visions of ecclesiastical ceremony conjured by the name Mitre Square, would quickly have been dispelled.

The square lay behind the church of St Katherine Cree in Leadenhall Street and was bounded by a couple of dwelling-houses, in one of which lived a City policeman. Only one of the three entrances to the square was wide enough for the carriages that called at the three large warehouses, the other entrances being pedestrian paths. In one of the provisions warehouses of Kearly & Tonge the night watchman paused in sweeping the staircase to make yet another cup of tea.

George Morris's years with the firm had accustomed him to the long night. He liked his own company – his days on the beat when he'd been in the force had taught him that – and there was always the odd visit from the patrolling policeman to while away ten minutes. His was a quiet square, and only occasionally would the silence be broken by the noise of a prowling cat or the steady rhythmic tread of a passing constable measuring the quarter hour.

The shrill scream of the whistling kettle was almost drowned by the pounding at the door. Outside, hammering frantically with his truncheon, stood the familiar figure of PC Watkins. The tall City constable grabbed the watchman's shoulders. 'For God's sake man come out and assist me; another woman has been ripped open!'

Morris tried to calm him, at the same time reaching beside the kettle for his matches. 'All right son, keep yourself cool while I light a lamp.' Already the constable was running back to the carriage entrance at the south-west corner of the square. His lamp beam shook as he motioned towards the dark shape lying in the shadows beside the railings. Morris raised his lantern and gasped in horror. Spreadeagled on the pavement, her shape marked out in blood, was the body of the woman.

Later, Morris would ask himself how this could have happened in the silence of the square – he had heard nothing. It was impossible that the victim could have screamed without him hearing her. However, unbeknown to Morris, the silence was not the most remarkable thing about this terrible crime: there was something else. Not five streets away a similarly nightmarish tableau had been presented – a killing of less than an hour before, as if in some grisly rehearsal of this butchery. The only difference was that at Berner Street the killer had been interrupted in his hellish purpose, whereas here, despite patrolling police, he had had time to carve his obscene trademark.

The woman's dress, with its gay pattern of Michaelmas daisies and golden lilies, had been pushed up to her waist and bunched up on her bosom together with her undergarments. Her stomach had been entirely laid open with a sharp knife. The intestines had been detached and were festooned about the right shoulder in a bloody, veined mass. More of the viscera adorned the victim's left arm.

The constable's wavering light picked up the great gash in the woman's throat and as Morris raised his lamp to her face he felt his churning stomach reach up to meet his throat. Her face had been all but hacked away.

Alternately shrieking and blowing his whistle the watchman ran southward towards the main entry to the square. More police arrived and about twenty minutes later – in a dash from Cloak Lane police station where he had been sleeping – came Major Henry Smith, the City of London Police Commissioner.

Although the majority of the enormous sprawl of the metropolis is watched over by the Metropolitan Police, there is an area just one mile square that is the jealous preserve of oft-times taller men, who wear a different uniform. They come under the control of the independent committee of aldermen, unlike their comrades in the Met., who answer directly to the Home Secretary. These are the City of London Police. In taking his deeds across the boundary in Aldgate to Mitre Square the Ripper had moved into their ancient domain.

The killer's escape route lay north from the square via Duke Street, across Houndsditch and Middlesex Street, back into Whitechapel and into Goulston Street. In a narrow close off nearby Dorset Street the little-known public sink still contained the blood where he had stopped to wash his hands. There was no doubt that the killer knew this labyrinth intimately.

Back in Goulston Street, Constable Alfred Long, a patrolling policeman, had discovered two important clues. First, he found a bloody piece of the victim's apron lying outside the doors of the flats which formed

Wentworth Dwellings. Inside these doors, at numbers 118 and 119, the constable came across a message that had been scrawled hastily upon the wall in white chalk.

THE JUWES ARE NOT THE
MEN THAT WILL BE BLAMED
FOR NOTHING

Some of the words appeared to be smeared with blood. It was 2.55 a.m. The constable knew that the clues had not been there thirty-five minutes earlier.

Whether, in retrospect, the fleeing killer would really stop in order to perform these graffiti, and considering the time inconsistencies, it may be that this 'clue' was nothing but a red herring, written coincidentally by some practical joker, or about another matter entirely. Be that as it may the writing was considered so important that no less a figure than Sir Charles Warren, Commissioner of the Met., was informed. Goulston Street lay back in the Metropolitan area and the divisional chief, Superintendent Arnold, fearing a riot, wanted the message rubbed out. A City detective restrained him, saying that he would wait by the evidence until daylight when a photograph could be taken. Sir Charles arrived at the scene at 5.00 a.m. It would be daylight in an hour. The Commissioner acted decisively.

Seven days later, at the inquest at Golden Lane mortuary, the mounting incredulity of the City Coroner can be gauged in this exchange with Major Smith:

'Why weren't the words photographed as you had ordered?'
'Someone in the Metropolitan Police ordered them washed away.'
'Who gave this order?'
'Sir Charles Warren, I am informed.'
'The Commissioner of the Metropolitan Police ordered that a message that might be in the killer's own hand was to be wiped away?'
'I believe it had something to do with his fear of anti-semitic rioting in Whitechapel.'
'Did you comment to the press that Sir Charles Warren had wiped the message clear with his own hand?'
'I was so informed.'

The court heard that various suggestions such as rubbing out only the top line, or the word 'Juwes', had been rejected by the Commissioner.

It was not long before the body was identified. Catherine Eddowes was well known to the police. She worked a small area of Whitechapel

Mitre Square, where Jack's crimes crossed the police boundary into the City of London. A priory had once stood on the site and local people were quick to recall an ancient curse.

and had in fact been in police custody less than an hour before she was killed, having been taken to Bishopsgate after being found lying drunk on a pavement in Aldgate. It was usual to allow drunks to sober up in the cells and then release them without punishment, and this is what had happened to Kate. Whatever the folly of letting a half-drunk woman on to the night-time city streets, Kate had left the police station singing loudly some time before one o'clock. From there to Mitre Square is about twenty-five minutes' walk. It was in these last fateful minutes that Kate met her killer.

The large, draughty mortuary building was crowded with witnesses, spectators, reporters and city officials. Fifty or more people thronged the long, dark gallery which formed the main room. The City Solicitor questioned Mrs Eliza Gold, who told a complicated tale about her sister's life. Kate had been married for eight years to Thomas Conway and had his initials tattooed on her arm. He had run off when she was about twenty-six. She had lived on and off at the notorious den of thieves and prostitutes at 55, Flower & Dean Street. Her latest 'husband' in common law was John Kelly. She sometimes used the name Kelly in pawnshops and other transactions.

John Kelly, a labourer, seems to have been genuinely fond of his paramour. He identified the body, and his evidence was punctuated with tears as he told of the final weeks of their seven years together. Each September the hopfields of Kent supplied work opportunities for Londoners, who would make the forty mile journey to pick the hops that went into beer-making. The pair had left London for the fields of Coxheath on 1 September.

The going rate was a shilling for seven bushels and Kate, as he called her, was unwell so they earned very little. It was at this time she made an extraordinary statement to Kelly. She claimed to know who the Ripper was. Reward money was being offered and with her knowledge their immediate financial problems could be solved. They had walked back to Whitechapel the previous Thursday. Their pathetic pennies had been shared to get lodgings separately and on the Saturday morning Eddowes had pawned Kelly's boots for half a crown to buy some food. Kelly walked barefoot.

However many criticisms are offered to the modern state welfare provisions, a glance back to the way in which our grandfathers ignored the poor heaps harsh judgment on the leaders of the wealthiest state in Europe.

Kelly's evidence completed, Dr Frederick Gordon Brown, Surgeon of the City of London Police, entered the witness box:

> The body was on its back, the head turned towards the left shoulder, and the arms were by its side as if they had fallen there. Both palms were upwards and the fingers slightly bent. A thimble was lying on the ground near the right hand. The clothes were drawn up, the left leg extended straight down and the right leg was bent at thigh and knee. There was a great disfigurement of the face. The throat was cut across and below the cut was a neckerchief. The upper part of the dress had been pulled open a little way. The abdomen was all exposed; the intestines were drawn out to a large extent and placed over the right shoulder; a piece of the intestine was quite detached from the body and placed between the left arm and the body. The lobe of the right ear was cut obliquely through, there was a quantity of clotted blood on the pavement. The body had been there only a few minutes.

The doctor gave more details and included his findings about the knife. Because it had hit gristle he could tell how the knife had made the cut. The knife was about six inches long. It was held so that it pointed towards the left side, with the handle towards the right. He considered that the killer had a good deal of anatomical knowledge of abdominal organs and ways to remove them. The cause of death was haemorrhage from the left common carotid artery. Death had been immediate.

Poor Kate. At forty-three she looked sixty. She was generally emaciated (Kelly's evidence was punctuated by references to gin, which contrasted strangely with the complete lack of any mention of food), and the pathologist forecast that she would have been dead from Bright's Disease within the year. Bright's Disease, a condition known as 'ginny kidney', is brought on by an excessive intake of alcohol. The pathologist had made his deductions from a single remaining kidney, for one had been removed. The authorities would receive a grisly reminder of this some days later.

Following the first murder, displeased with the progress of the police, tradesmen had formed themselves into the Whitechapel Vigilance Committee to offer mutual protection and reward for information leading to the apprehension of the murderer. Their chairman was a Mile End builder named George Lusk. A few days after Kate Eddowes murder the chairman found himself the recipient of a most unwelcome package. A cardboard box, containing what appeared to be a human kidney, arrived at his office, with the following unpunctuated letter:

> From Hell
> Mr Lusk sir I send you half the kidne I took from one woman prasarved for you tother piece I fried and ate it was very nise I may send you the bloody knif that took it out if you only wate a whil longer.
> Signed. *Catch me when you can Mishter Lusk.*

Lusk forwarded the revolting object to Major Smith, who had it examined by two pathologists. Dr Openshaw, pathological curator of the London Hospital Museum proclaimed the kidney to be that of a woman of about forty-five in an advanced state of Bright's Disease. The kidney had been placed in spirits shortly after its removal. Another independent examination by a Dr Reed produced the same findings.

Newspapers scoffed at what was seen as a hoax, but the public laughter petered out when Major Smith revealed that the posted kidney had one inch of renal artery attached. A female human renal artery is about three inches long. Two inches had been found in the corpse.

Murders of Liz Stride and Catherine Eddowes: description of main suspects

Following the double-murder more suspects descriptions were published:

> Middling height. Black coat, light trousers, middle-aged, rather stout. A round cap with small peak like a sailor. Clean, respectable, like a clerk. No whiskers (but face obscured). Nothing carried, no stick. Mild, educated voice.
> (Man seen at 11.45 p.m. Saturday. Witness William Marshall, 60, Berner St, warehouseman. At inquest, and three others.)

> Cut away dark coat – down to his heels. Hat – not known. 5 ft 7 in. Not very stout. Parcel in newspaper 18 in × 6 in. Dark felt deerstalker. Age twenty-eight. No whiskers.
>
> (PC Smith, H Division)

> Thirty years old, 5 ft 9 in in height, small fair moustache, dressed in something like navy serge and with deerstalker's hat, peak fore and aft. He also wore a red handkerchief.
> (Man seen talking to Eddowes ten minutes before her death. Witness Lawende, commercial traveller, at inquest. It was a bright moonlit night – Major Smith, Commissioner City of London Police considered description accurate.)
>
> At 1.35 a.m. on 30 September, with Catherine Eddowes, in Church Passage leading to Mitre Square, where she was found murdered at 1.45 a.m. same date, a man age thirty, height 5 ft 7 or 8 in; complexion fair, moustache fair, medium build, dress – pepper and salt colour, loose jacket, grey cloth cap with peak of same material, reddish neckerchief tied in knot, appearance of a sailor.
>
> (*Police Gazette*)

> At 12.35 a.m., 30 September, with Elizabeth Stride, found murdered on same date in Berner Street at 1.00 a.m., a man, age twenty-eight, height 5 ft 8 in, complexion dark, small dark moustache; dress – black diagonal coat, hard felt hat, collar and tie, respectable appearance, carried a parcel wrapped in newspaper.
> At 12.45 a.m., 30 September with the same woman in Berner Street, a man, age about thirty, height about 5 ft 5 in, complexion fair, hair dark, small brown moustache, full face, broad shoulders. Dress – dark jacket and trousers, black cap with peak.'
>
> (*Police Gazette*)

8

Warren's Rabbits

Dr PETER WARREN OF TORQUAY was astonished, aggrieved and deeply hurt at the treatment of his grandfather by the *Radio Times*, but when he protested to the Editor, in July 1983, he received scant sympathy. The writer Elwyn Jones retorted:

> The television programmes have already made it clear that Sir Charles Warren was a great public-order man. All the energies he used to solve those horrible crimes included the destruction of potentially valuable evidence: the writing on the wall.

Was the military man's great sense of public-order such that everything else including sensible criminal investigation assumed lower priority? There is no doubt that in the powerful position he occupied during his two and a half years as police commissioner there had been very serious problems of civil unrest which he had dealt with firmly. Some said ruthlessly. He had held command of the Diamond Fields Horse Brigade in the Kaffir war ten years before and his experience in putting down native rebellion was seen by many to be inappropriate when used in Trafalgar Square.

The beginning of autumn in 1887 had seen large numbers of unemployed workers camping out in the parks around the West End. Frequently the crowd would assemble into noisy advertisement of the unemployment problem. Shopkeepers were fed up with the ragged bands and had threatened to form vigilante patrols. With the Home Secretary's approval Warren closed Trafalgar Square on certain days.

Fears of mob rule were realized shortly after this when the homeless, denied the square, gathered beneath the statue of Nelson and fought a pitched battle with police. The thirteenth of November would be remembered as Bloody Sunday.

The mob was armed with iron bars, knives, and anything else that came to hand. Warren assembled his troops, several hundred Grenadier and Life Guards, 300 constables and mounted police. In the mêlée that followed more than 150 of the crowd were treated for injuries and almost 300 arrested.

Warren's vigorous control of the crowd won only a short victory, for the unemployed became more inflamed and there were more riots and increasing political comment. A year later, at the height of the Whitechapel crimes, David Lloyd George, young and still striving to achieve a seat in parliament, attacked the police: 'such harrowing of the poor dockers and denying of the rights of strikers while failing miserably to find the brute who kills the poor women in the East End.'

Most historians seem to consider that the unimaginative, authoritarian Warren was a most unfortunate choice for commissioner, especially at this sensitive time. He brought little relevant experience to the post and upset and antagonized those below and above him, including the Home Secretary and eventually the Queen herself.

The Home Office, which had ultimate control of the Met., was run by civilians, a situation that offended Warren's military background. His annual reports are said to have been devoid of reference to criminal matters in preference to discussion about horses for police.

Although his middle and later years seemed marred by promotions for which his qualities of military leadership were inadequate, as a young man he had gained considerable credibility. His archaeological pursuits had resulted in such works as *Underground Jerusalem* (1874). His military career had included an important role as commissioner for the settlement of the boundaries between the Orange Free State and Griqualand West two years later. He had conducted the very successful Bechuanaland expedition the year before becoming Chief Commissioner of the Metropolitan Police in 1886. But had this hitherto distinguished career really prepared the forty-six year old Welshman for his role as leader of the police force in the world's largest city?

The previous holder of the post, Sir Edward Henderson, had also been a soldier. His resignation followed criticism of his military-style handling of a street riot in Pall Mall and the West End. There were those who saw Warren's appointment as a curious choice following the departure of his military predecessor. Others observed that Salisbury, the Prime Minister, was a member of the Brotherhood of Freemasons, and in his appointment of Warren he had not only one of England's highest-ranking Masons but one of the most powerful in the world. The District Grand Master of the Eastern Archipelago, with three Lodges in South Africa named after him, the founder in England of the Quatuor Coronati Lodge of Masonic Research and Past Grand Sojourner in the Supreme Grand Chapter now had yet another title: Chief Commissioner of the Metropolitan Police.

Not for the first time (and certainly not the last, as events in our

Sir Charles Warren. His resignation over differences of opinion about the organization of the Detective Department left him a discredited and defeated man. Why had the killer proved so elusive?

recent times have shown), the public were distrustful of the fact that many leading police officers were Freemasons. Could the Masonic connection explain his appointment? Henderson had not been a Mason. With his replacement a Brotherhood duo of Salisbury and Warren had been formed.

Under Warren's hand the reputation of the police, already low following a corruption scandal a few years before, was not enhanced. Newspaper reports, daily, leave little doubt that by the end of 1887 Warren had fallen far from public acclaim, and yet it was at this time that he was awarded a knighthood.

So it was with the addition of another title that Sir Charles Warren began 1888. A year of extraordinary blunders that left a city in turmoil and five mutilated corpses.

The beginning of the year was marked by a deterioration in the relationship between the Home Secretary and the Commissioner. The quarrels between Henry Matthews and Warren that had begun the previous year worsened. Their arguments ranged over matters of discipline, crowd control and the right of the Home Secretary to apply the Official Secrets Act to the police and its Commissioner. Matthews was an able lawyer, but he had few talents in personnel matters and caused trouble between Warren and his subordinates. Munro had been head of CID for four years and claimed to be independent of Warren. Matters worsened and Warren forced Munro's resignation in August 1888. Anderson then replaced Munro. With the appointment of Anderson the duo became a Masonic Triumvirate.

The public had little faith in the police. The Whitechapel Vigilance Committee gained in strength and letters were sent to the Queen. Throughout the autumn the public's general disquiet grew. Public meetings were called and thousands attended, passing resolutions demanding the resignation of the Commissioner.

Warren racked his brains. His list of measures had included consideration of plans to equip the constables with rubber-soled shoes to silence their approach on the cobbled streets, and dressing his officers as street-women as bait for the Ripper.

Victoria's London gave any alert criminal a good run. Telephones, less than ten years old, were not in general use. The quickest communication was by telegram. There were no mobile police in fast vehicles. Sometimes a criminal would make the mistake of dashing away by train and the police could head him off by telegram, but if he stayed in London a criminal knew he was on equal terms with the authorities. He could run as fast as they could. Their hansom cab was no faster than his.

Warren badly needed something to give him the edge. Then his eyes lighted on a letter in *The Times*.

Within days of Elizabeth Stride's murder in the club yard at Berner Street, the press had been bombarded with offers of help from bloodhound owners. *The Times* recalled that a murderer in Blackburn in 1876 had been traced by such a dog. Senior police officers were appalled when their chief took the idea seriously. A subsequent commissioner of the Met., Sir Melville Macnaghten, later wrote:

> It should have been obvious that bloodhounds were useless in Whitechapel. I cannot conceive of a more impossible locality in which to expect hounds to work. A highly placed police official arranged to be hunted himself by bloodhounds in Hyde Park. He had begun to think that the police were on the way to becoming the masters.
>
> (*Days of my Years*, Sir Melville Macnaghten, Edward Arnold, 1915)

Warren obtained a pair of champion hounds, Burgho and Barnaby from Edwin Brough, a well-known bloodhound breeder of Scarborough. They were brought to London but with little success. Many hours were spent training the dogs; Warren is said to have played the part of the quarry himself, and the hounds pursued him enthusiastically, but the commissioner lost them. The next day on Tooting Common they could not be found and had to be tracked down by police. With every police station alerted police credibility sank lower and press comment was derisive. The public attitude was tersely summed up on 13 November by a *Star* editorial:

> Sir Charles Warren may now be reconciled to his bloodhounds. These animals, it will be remembered, mysteriously disappeared, and there is no doubt that, finding they could not get on with the Chief Commissioner, they resigned

A *Times* reader suggested noiseless bicycle patrols by day and night would be useful, but the authorities did not act and it was left to the constables' own initiative to silence their footsteps, usually with strips of rubber tyre nailed clumsily to their boots. The senior officers' plans seemed so disorganized to the constables, who considered themselves misused by their superiors, that one was moved to state that they were all 'Warren's rabbits'.

The Home Secretary was under attack from all sides. Rumours of public disquiet and murmurs of discontent in the police ranks daily grew more insistent. Reported sightings of Jack the Ripper in the streets of San Francisco and the diamond fields of South Africa kept the story alive in the world press, and home and foreign newspapers compared the activities of the Met. unfavourably with those of the City force, which had been brought into the drama by the events in Mitre Square.

The final straw for Matthews came when in the November issue of *Murray's Magazine* Warren wrote about the difficulties of policing when the criminal investigation department was independent of the Commissioner of Police.

In the difficult atmosphere that existed between the Commissioner and the Home Secretary, Warren found himself increasingly shut out from communication between the Home Office and the CID. Warren was in an invidious position; under attack he was being kept short of vital information. But to go public with internal police business! Matthews was furious – wasn't Warren aware of the rule that forbade discussions in the press by serving police officers? On 8 November Warren tendered his resignation. Matthews accepted. Jack's victims didn't always bleed.

9
Mary

A T THE BEGINNING OF THE 1860s a number of narrow streets thickly populated with thieves, prostitutes and beggars were removed. Essex Street and Old Rose Lane disappeared and the broad span of New Commercial Street was built, linking Shoreditch to the London Docks, cutting across Whitechapel, and in particular, through the midst of a densely populated area.

It could have been an opportunity for change. Indeed there were a few social reformers who tried to encourage the spread of respectable lodgings, at the same time discouraging the majority of disreputable establishments. It was a forlorn task. Spitalfields had been a notorious rookery for infamous characters for more than two centuries, and as the navvies cut their thoroughfare, sweeping courts, alleys and tenements before them, so the human flotsam merely regrouped on either side of New Commercial Street.

By the time of the Whitechapel murders, Spitalfields rookery was as firmly established as it had been before the planners' improvements. Four hundred square yards was home to eight hundred thieves, vagabonds, beggars and whores, most of whom had lived previously in the notorious Essex Street and Old Rose Lane.

From George Yard, where Martha Tabram had been found, over Wentworth Street and past the roads and alleys whose names feature in all the crimes – Thrawl Street, Flower & Dean Street, Fashion Street – the new road cut its way northward, slashing a great scar through the heart of Whitechapel.

Towards the south of Spitalfields Market was one of the most dangerous thieves' hideouts; coiners' dens were in every street, and publicans frequently doubled as receivers of stolen goods. In small yards and skittle grounds behind the taverns, fighting dogs were chained to kennels before entering wooden enclosures to kill rats or each other. The audience for these events could number as many as a hundred, all coarse and brutal in appearance. Many would be known to each other, partners in crime. Here a stranger walked at his peril and could not hope to go unnoticed. Many areas of this part of Spitalfields were considered so dangerous that even the men of H Division would not venture in alone.

In the very centre of this purlieu, opposite Flower & Dean Street with its dozens of threepence-a-night lodgings and bordering the vast meat market at Spitalfields, was Dorset Street, a narrow road with barely sufficient room for two carriages to pass. Not that many carriages came this way – the odd coster-barrow, perhaps – but the swells in their hansoms didn't loiter here. Virtually all the houses provided lodgings for people who would come late at night, to disappear again, mostly to illegal pursuits, during the day.

Off Dorset Street, a brick tunnel about three feet wide formed a miserable dark alley extending twenty feet from the street into a small yard barely fifteen feet wide. This was Miller's Court. On the corner of the court, running the length of the alley and fronting Dorset Street, was McCarthy's chandler's shop, which gave the place its local name 'McCarthy's Rents'. John McCarthy owned two of the six mean houses in the court.

The houses in Dorset Street backed on to the court, through which occupants of the rear rooms would enter. One such place was number twenty-six Dorset Street, whose ground floor had been partitioned to form number thirteen Miller's Court, a dismal, sparsely-furnished room which was rented by Mary Jane Kelly.

Mary had occupied the room since the previous March. Although described as the lowest form of prostitute Mary must have had some redeeming qualities, for not only had she kept the room for some eight months, she had even been allowed by her landlord to fall into arrears with the rent. This was an area where many rents were collected by the day, but Mary was obviously held in some trust by McCarthy for she owed twenty-nine shillings, four weeks' rent.

The indefatigable Ripper investigator Donald Rumbelow, author of *The Complete Jack the Ripper* (W. H. Allen, 1975), has observed that as the majority of women in McCarthy's rents were prostitutes it is possible that the money was more than just rent payment. Even so, it was a considerable amount to have outstanding.

In a part of London riddled with disease and poverty Mary shone like a beacon. A Celtic beauty, with raven black waist-length hair and blue eyes, her bearing and youthful attractiveness made her a remarkable and instantly recognizable figure in the area. She was short, about 5 ft 3 in, and attractively rounded, if a little plump. The paths of prostitution that had brought her from Ireland to Cardiff, to the bordellos of Haymarket (she claimed) and a paramour in Paris had ended, temporarily at least, in the cesspool that was Miller's Court.

POLICE THE ILLUSTRATED NEWS

LAW COURTS AND WEEKLY RECORD

No. 1,292.   SATURDAY, NOVEMBER 17, 1888.   Price One Penny.

SKETCHES OF THE SEVENTH EAST END CRIME.

PHOTOGRAPHING THE BODY.

REMOVING THE BODY TO SHOREDITCH MORTUARY.

A MYSTERIOUS MAN WITH A BLACK BAG.

FORCING OPEN THE DOOR.

THREE TIMES ARRESTED JACK THE RIPPER.

THE SEVENTH HORRIBLE MURDER BY THE MONSTER OF THE EAST-END.

MILLER'S COURT. THE MURDERER'S CHOSEN SPOT.

MY PRAYERS LAST LEAVE TAKING OF THE VICTIM.

STRANGE MAN TRIED TO INDUCE GIRL TO GO AND GET ENTRY WITH HIM.

LURED TO THE SLAUGHTER.

SCENE WITNESSED BY THE POLICE.

THE ILLUSTRATED POLICE NEWS OFFERS £100 REWARD FOR THE CAPTURE OF THE WHITECHAPEL MURDERER.

WINDOWS BOARDED UP.

THE SCENE OF THE MURDER. MILLER'S COURT.

THE AWFUL DISCOVERY BY McCARTHY.

THE SEVENTH VICTIM! PICKED OUT FOR SLAUGHTER BY THE EAST-END FIEND. FROM DESCRIPTIONS GIVEN BY HER INTIMATE FRIENDS.

STARTLING STORY OF A MAN WITH A BLACK BAG.

ANOTHER STRANGE STORY TOLD OF A MAN WITH A BLACK BAG.

THE MURDERER ESCAPING FROM THE WINDOW.

ARRESTED ON SUSPICION.

LOCALITY OF THE SEVEN UNDISCOVERED MURDERS.

REMOVING THE BODY.

Mary's room was about twelve feet square and contained a few sticks of shabby rented furniture comprising an iron bedstead, two rickety tables and a single chair. Torn muslin served as curtains at the broken window that looked out on to the court.

Here Mary lived with a man she called her husband, Joseph Kelly. In fact he was Joseph Barnett, a kindly enough man who had picked her up in Commercial Street nearly two years before. They had instantly agreed to live together, and this they had done, with occasional tiffs, such as the one in which the window had got broken, until 30 October, nine days before.

There had been rumours that Mary was involved in the considerable sapphism that abounded amongst her calling – certainly she would have been aware of the clubs in the West End that catered for such women. There were those who said that her intimacies with a woman called Maria Harvey, who lived at New Court off Dorset Street, went beyond that of friendly neighbours who shared a pipe or two at the Britannia. Such behaviour was commonplace enough among certain of her kind and was taken very much for granted. 'Wearing queer drawers' would scarcely have raised an eyebrow in those squalid streets. Even so, it was scarcely surprising that Joe Barnett should object. When Maria moved in, Joe moved out.

For Mary, one Thursday was much like any other. She would have numerous penny drinks at the Britannia, fatigued after her day-time meetings with customers, unbeknown to Joe, who was at the market. Later she would stagger home on Joe's arm, at about one o'clock in the morning.

Last night had been different. It was more than a week since Joe had stormed off to his sister's place in Gray's Inn Road. Mary missed him. She was sure he'd be back, he was a good man and cared for her. Why, only that evening he'd called in to tell her he was sorry not to have any money for her, work being what it was. He'd be back, she was sure. Meanwhile, the night was still young. She could hear the clock on St Stephen's at Spitalfields. It was two o'clock.

Mary tossed her long, narrow, red cape over her shoulders; it hung to the floor, covering the shabby skirt and velvet top. The coat was getting difficult to button – at three months pregnant her waist was filling out rapidly.

It was raining lightly as Mary crossed New Commercial Street and

Miller's Court gave the *Illustrated Police News* a 'seventh' victim. The alley entrance is beside the door to room thirteen, its small window boarded up after police removal of the frame.

she scarcely noticed the short stout figure with the black hat at the corner of Thrawl Street. His voice was soft. 'Hello Mary.'

'Hullo Hutchinson,' Mary smiled, 'Just the man I wanted to see. I'm so down. Will you lend me a tanner?'

Hutchinson laughed, a hollow empty laugh that sent his breath steaming on the cold night air. 'Sixpence? I haven't even enough for a bed for meself. I've been in Romford all day and there's bugger all work down there for anyone. I'd help if I could – but I can't.'

Mary smiled at him again. 'Sure, I know you would. Ah well, good morning to you. I must go and find some money.' She turned away and began to walk towards Thrawl Street. Hutchinson stood and watched her; he'd known Mary for three years and had a soft spot for the likable, vivacious Irish charmer. She had not gone more than a dozen steps when a man coming towards her stopped and put his hand on her arm. They paused for a moment and the man put his arm around her as they walked back towards Hutchinson. The curled ends of the stranger's moustache bobbed up and down as the couple shared some laughter.

The man was about thirty-five, not much taller than Mary – about 5 ft 6 in – and Hutchinson felt distinctly uneasy about him. From his high-button boots and spats to the horseshoe pin flashing in his black tie, he looked a mite too smartly togged out for Whitechapel. The long, dark coat was expensively trimmed at collar and cuffs with astrakhan, and beneath it a heavy gold chain dangled from the light waistcoat, to end in a shimmering red jewel that glowed in the gaslight like the eye of some tormented animal.

Hutchinson tried to look at the stranger's face as they passed him, but the man pulled his soft felt hat further over his eyes, shielding his face with a thin parcel about eight inches long and wrapped in dark shiny American cloth. In his right hand he carried a pair of brown kid gloves.

They stood talking at the corner of Miller's Court and Hutchinson followed at a distance. Mary's voice rippled clearly in the cold night air.

'All right my dear, come along, you'll be comfortable.'

The man leaned over and kissed her. Hutchinson watched Mary straighten up, complaining that she had lost her handkerchief. With a flourish the stranger produced a red one and pressed it into her hand. They linked arms and made their way into the court. Hutchinson assumed that they had gone into Mary's room, number thirteen.

What prompted Hutchinson to wait he couldn't tell. He was uneasy;

Miller's Court. The sole entrance from Dorset Street, a lane of common lodgings. The chair belongs to an old woman who for many years charged a fee to morbid sightseers.

he had nowhere to go for the night and was curious to see when the stranger would leave, but after three-quarters of an hour with the cold November wind tugging at his thin jacket, Hutchinson called it a night. He left just before 3 a.m.

In the chandler's shop on the corner of Miller's Court a round figure was stacking boxes. It was almost 11 a.m., and Thomas Bowyer had been at the task since the shop had opened some hours before. Behind the counter John McCarthy was checking the cash drawer and muttering angrily about outstanding money. He pushed the drawer shut noisily and looked up at his assistant.

'Tom. Go round to number thirteen, ask Mary Jane for the rent and don't take no for an answer.'

Bowyer straightened up, it was a welcome break from the morning's work. He liked Mary and it wasn't the first time he'd called for the rent, but there was often a problem.

The sun was shining brightly as he stepped out of the shop and down the alley into Miller's Court. A small group of shabbily dressed men squatted on the concrete paving playing pitch and toss, coins changing hands and anxious heads turning this way and that, wary of any police approach.

Bowyer knocked at the faded door; he watched the gamblers idly for a moment and then turned back to the door. He knocked again, harder. He tried the handle, but it was locked. It crossed his mind that Mary was expecting his errand and might be ignoring his knocking. Just around the corner was a window in four quarters. He peered through the grimy glass but the curtains were drawn. The lower of the four panes, the one nearest the door, was broken. Gingerly, Bowyer put his hand through and lifted the tattered muslin.

In the chandler's shop McCarthy licked his pencil as he put the finishing touches to a column of figures in the narrow ledger. He paused and looked around him. This morning was quiet. The annual Lord Mayor's Show was taking place and the side streets around Spitalfields were deserted as their inhabitants massed in the main street to watch the procession. Golden coaches didn't often visit, but today the new Lord Mayor would pass through on his journey from the Mansion House to the Guildhall for the swearing-in.

McCarthy's shop door was open and he could hear the crowds in Leadenhall Street singing and shouting. Suddenly the dishevelled figure of his assistant appeared in the doorway. Pale, shaking and wild-eyed, he swayed and steadied himself against the door. 'Guv'nor, guv'nor, come quick, number thirteen. Oh my God. Jack the . . .'

He clamped his hand over his mouth and reeled into the street. McCarthy ran after him, down the passage and into the court. Bowyer pointed speechlessly to the window and McCarthy whisked aside the curtain.

In the gloom of the unlit interior he could see the shape on the bed. As his eyes adjusted from the bright sunlight its form became clearer and the horror of the scene drew sharply into focus. A mass of raw flesh, like some butcher's carcass, lay stretched upon the bed. That it had been human could be made out only from the shape, for the face had been skinned, the ears and nose had been cut off, and the head hung sideways, grotesquely severed by the deep slash that had rent the throat from ear to ear.

The remains of a linen undergarment clung to the corpse. The abdomen had been ripped partially open and both breasts had been cut from the body. Like the head, the left arm hung to the body by the skin only. The thighs down to the feet had been stripped of flesh and McCarthy could see the leg bones gleaming white. The abdomen had been slashed across and downward and most of the internal organs removed. One arm and hand had been plunged into the mess that had been her stomach. Blood had spurted across three of the four walls and lay in a pool beneath the body and under the bed.

McCarthy felt his pulse hammering in his temples. Draped around the room from every picture rail the bloody entrails hung suspended like some awful yuletide decoration. The final horror struck the grocer as his eyes lighted on the table beside the corpse. He retched violently, for there neatly piled on the scrubbed wooden surface he could see kidneys, breasts and heart.

10
Letters from Hell

DEAR BOSS,
I keep hearing the police have caught me, but they won't fix me
just yet. I have laughed when they look so clever and talk about
being on the right track. The joke about the leather apron gives me
real fits.

I am down on whores and I shan't stop ripping them till I do get
buckled. Grand work, the last job was. I gave the lady no time to
squeal. How can they catch me now? I love my work and want to
start again. You will soon hear of me and my funny little games.
The next job I do I shall clip the layds (sic) ears off and send them
to the police, just for jolly, wouldn't you?

Jack the Ripper

Beneath the signature was added:

Don't mind me giving the trade name. Wasn't good enough to post
this before I got all the red ink off my hands: curse it. No luck yet.
They say I am a doctor now. Ha, ha.

Among the thousands of Ripper-related letters that were sent to the
police, the Vigilance Committee or the London Hospital, this letter
stands out. The postmark showed that it had been posted in east
London on 28 September, two days before the murder of Catherine
Eddowes. The date fixes clearly that the reference to mutilation of the
ears (it hadn't happened before) was part of the programme. A chance
guess on the part of a crank? Perhaps, but written two days before a
murder in which the victim's ears had been slashed?

The name Jack the Ripper started at this point. Assuming that the
writer and the murderer are one and the same, then the invention of the
name that has gone down in history must be accorded to the murderer
himself. The letter had been addressed to 'The Boss, Central News
Office, London City.' and was published in *The Times* on 3 October.
Meanwhile the CNA had received the following postcard, postmarked
30 September:

I was not codding, dear old Boss, when I gave you the tip. You'll hear about Saucy Jack's work tomorrow. Double event this time.
Number One squealed a bit. Couldn't finish straight off. Had no time to get ears for police. Thanks for keeping last letter back till I go to work again.

Jack the Ripper

In his book *The Identity of Jack the Ripper* (Jarrold, 1959), Donald McCormick pointed out that this was a Sunday and nothing was published until a day later. The East End would have been awash with rumour, but the writer knew so many specifics. Was the squeal he referred to the same stifled cry heard by the Stride inquest witness, Mrs

Mortimer? There had been an attempt to remove the ears. The reference to the as yet unpublished letter also gives grounds for supposing this to be genuine. Police checked the possibility that a pressman, perhaps at the CNA, might have written the second letter with knowledge of the first, but they found no proof.

It was shortly after this that the portion of kidney, accompanied by a letter, was sent to Mr Lusk.

One of the problems facing the police was the sheer volume of correspondence from far and wide. It was as if half the population was bent on sending practical jokes or well-meant but half-baked ideas to the authorities. Letters were arriving from overseas, newspaper clippings of sightings and confessions came with every post, and the meagre administrative resources of Scotland Yard were strained to breaking-point. The Yard took the unprecedented step of printing a ready-made acknowledgment letter, which relieved some of the work, but precious manpower and time still had to be spent sifting the information.

In the midst of the postal avalanche came one letter bearing the royal crest. Queen Victoria was known not to suffer fools gladly, and the aging monarch (she was sixty-nine), expressed a shrewd knowledge of what was happening just three miles east of Buckingham Palace:

> The Queen fears that the detective department is not so efficient as it might be. No doubt the recent murders in Whitechapel were committed in circumstances which made detection very difficult; still, the Queen thinks that, in the small area where these horrible crimes have been perpetuated, a great number of detectives might be employed and that every possible suggestion might be carefully examined, and, if practicable, followed.
>
> Have the cattle boats and passenger boats been examined? Has any investigation been made as to the number of single men occupying rooms to themselves? The murderer's clothes must be saturated with blood and kept somewhere. Is there sufficient surveillance at night?
>
> These are some of the questions that occur to the Queen on reading the accounts of these horrible crimes.

The Home Secretary's unofficial reaction can only be guessed at. What is certain is that more pressure was put on Warren and his men.

The astute suggestion about shipping movements caused meticulous checks to be carried out, especially on the monthly cattle boats that usually docked just before a weekend and left again on Sundays. The fact that the killings had taken place at weekends and that most crew would include a butcher, had not escaped the monarch.

This letter from Buckingham Palace throws an interesting and paradoxical light on the aged Queen, so often pictured as a black-costumed widow, a semi-recluse. The Queen had clearly spent time pondering the moves of the mysterious murderer. These pertinent comments on the crimes make it far more likely that each new account was devoured with Her Majesty's morning toast and that the royal marmalade was more than once spilled on the lurid woodcuts that adorned the weekly *Illustrated Police News*.

The newspapers did their best to keep their readers informed, though one wonders how much reassurance the readers of the *Daily Telegraph* would have gained from this report of the measures taken for their well-being:

> Shortly before midnight these assassin-hunters are dispatched upon their mission. Their footfall is silenced by the use of galoshes and their safety is assured by the carrying of police whistles and stout sticks.

Newspaper editors were kept busy with a torrent of readers' comment:

> '. . . disguise your officers as women . . .'
> '. . . armour plated collars to be knife-proof . . .'
> '. . . electric alarm bells in every street . . .'
> '. . . mechanical man-traps in female form, whose spring-loaded arms seize the suspect while the machine declares its triumph by loud blasts on a police whistle.'

Contemporary Ripperologist, Dr A. Forbes-Winslow, suggested an advertisement in the personal column:

> Gentleman who is strongly opposed to presence of fallen women in the streets of London would like to cooperate with someone with a view to their suppression.

Not that all readers were amateur sleuths, some kept their comments to sociological matters. The Rector of St Jude's Church, Commercial Street, Revd Samuel Barnett, wanted brothels to be purchased by philanthropists and converted into homes and night-refuges.

Ten days after the double murder, Revd R. C. Bedford, Bishop Suffrage for east London, wrote to *The Times*. He had been Rector of Spitalfields and was writing to protest at this well-meant suggestion:

> Another night-refuge is not required. It would attract more of these women into the neighbourhood and increase the difficulties of the situation. But what is needed is a home where washing and other work could be done and where poor women who are really anxious to lead a better life could find employment.
> There are penitentiaries and mission houses into which the

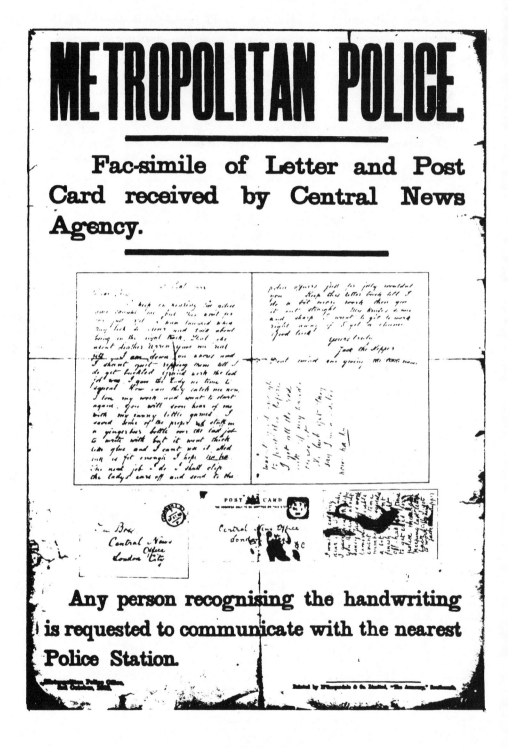

younger women can be received. The public generally are little aware of how much good work is being done of late among these. But for the older women, many of whom have only taken to their miserable mode of earning a living in sheer despair and who would gladly renounce it, we have not the home, it is of the utmost importance one should be provided. It would differ from the ordinary penitentiary. Two thousand pounds would enable the experiment to be tried, and I have no doubt at all of it being a success.

The Bishop went on to offer to conduct such a home and asked that volunteer ladies with charitable intentions should contact him.

It is my bounden duty to use my position and experience to turn to the best account the painful interest that has been excited by late events in the East End.

The letters column in *The Times* was bursting. From the Bishopsgate Rectory the Revd William Rogers suggested that prostitutes should be licensed:

I know the cry that will be raised against this, but I ask, are the interests of society to be sacrificed for a blatant prudery? Once registered, the women could be visited and attempts made to redeem them . . .

While willing to undertake these house-calls himself, Revd Rogers conceded that his position might make this task open to critical comment.

The clergy was not alone. Eminent drama critic, socialist and tireless newspaper letter writer George Bernard Shaw commented in the *Star*:

Sir, Will you allow me to make a comment on the success of the Whitechapel murderer in calling attention for a moment to the social question? Less than a year ago the West End press were literally clamouring for the blood of the people – hounding-on Sir Charles Warren to thrash and muzzle the scum who dared to complain that they were starving.

Quite lost on these journals were indignant remonstrances, arguments, speeches and sacrifices, appeals to history, philosophy, biology, economics and statistics, investigations into the condition of the unemployed, all unanswered and unanswerable. The press was still, frankly, for hanging the appellants.

Now all is changed. Private enterprise has succeeded where Socialism failed. Whilst we conventional Social Democrats were wasting our time on education, agitation and organization, some independent genius has taken the matter in hand, and by simply

murdering and disembowelling four women, converted the pro-
prietary press to an inept sort of Communism.

The moral is a pretty one. Dynamitards and anarchists will not
be slow to draw it. 'Humanity, political science, economics and
religion,' they will say, 'are all rot; the one argument that touches
your lady and gentleman is the knife.'

The Docks Strike riots of 1886 brought in £78,000 and a
People's Palace: it remains to be seen how much these murders
may prove worth to the East End. Indeed, if the habits of
duchesses only admitted of their being decoyed into Whitechapel
backyards, a single experiment in slaughter-house anatomy on an
aristocratic victim, might bring in a round half a million and save
the necessity of sacrificing four women of the people.

The Ripper murders were certainly spotlighting social problems in the
East End and the appalling social divide between rich and poor. The
remarkable statement made by the foreman of the jury at the inquest on
Polly Nichols, was to be heard on many lips. He had complained:

If it had been a rich person that was murdered there would have
been a reward of £1000 offered, but as it was only a poor
unfortunate hardly any notice was taken. I will myself give £25 for
the capture of the murderer.

On 16 November, after the Kelly murder, a *Times* editorial reported the
public reproofs that had been poured on the police. It called on the
community to assist the police and commented:

There is much more profitable occupation than vague windy abuse
of people who cannot create evidence. Deep searching of hearts,
humiliation of spirit, and sorrowful reflection over the causes
which make these unspeakable atrocities possible, would be more
seemly than cheap declamation about the shortcomings of the
police.

Others soon took up the cry. A petition was sent to the Queen by the
Whitechapel Vigilance Committee entreating her to offer a reward for
the capture of the killer. The Home Secretary steadfastly refused to
become involved in payments, but the Lord Mayor of London and the
aldermen in their square mile jurisdiction of the City had no such
reservations and, following the Eddowes murder, published the following notice:

Whereas at 1.45 a.m. on Sunday, 30 September a woman, name
unknown, was found brutally murdered in Mitre Square, Aldgate,
in this City.

A reward of £500 will be paid by the Commissioner of Police of
the City of London to any such person (other than a person

belonging to the Police Forces of the United Kingdom) who shall give such information as shall lead to the discovery and conviction of the murderer or murderers.

Information to be given to the Inspector of the Detective Department, 26, Old Jewry, or any police station.

James Fraser, Colonel, Commissioner,
City of London Police Office, 1 Oct 1888

Private offers of rewards came in from many quarters. The *Financial News* at the behest of its readers wrote to the Home Secretary:

In view of your refusal to offer a reward out of Government funds for the discovery of the perpetrator, or perpetrators, of the recent murders in the East End of London, I am instructed on behalf of several readers of the *Financial News*, whose names and addresses I enclose, to forward to you the accompanying cheque for £300, and to request you to offer that sum for this purpose, in the name of the Government.

The Home Office, returning the cheque, replied acerbically;

If Mr Matthews had been of the opinion that the offer of reward in these cases would have been attended by any useful result he would himself have at once made such an offer, but he is not of that opinion. Under these circumstances I am directed to return you the cheque (which I enclose) and to thank you and the gentlemen for the liberality of their offer which Mr Matthews much regrets he is unable to accept.

The prompt action of the Lord Mayor had been received with general satisfaction. The City reward, when added to the £400 offered by two newspapers, £100 from Mr Montague Hall MP, and £200 collected by the Vigilance Committee put a price of £1,200 on the killer's head. If, a century later, we add two noughts to this figure, some idea of the enormity of the reward can be measured.

The Lord Mayor had been urged to open a subscription list, and even the normally self-occupied and imperturbable members of the Stock Exchange had seemed disposed to take up the matter.

The newspaper readers had again been treated to a demonstration of division within the authorities. While this wrangling was taking place, Jack's own pen was still busy:

From Hell Mr Lusk
sir   I send you half the kidne i took from one woman prasarved for you tother piece I fried and ate it was very nise I may send you the bloody knif that took it out if you only wate a whil longer.
Signed. *Catch me when you can Mishter Lusk.*

Thirteen days later, on 29 October, a letter was sent to the doctor who had examined the kidney.

> Old Boss, you was rite it was the lift kidny; i was goin to hopperate again close to your ospittle – just as i was goin to drop my nife along of er blooming throte them cusses of coppers spoilt the game but i guess i will be on the job soon and will send you another bit of innerds.

> *Jack the Ripper*

> O have you seen the devle with his mikerscope and scalpul a-lookin at a kidney with a slide cocked up.

The phoneticism of this missive predated by some forty years the peculiar notions of Hollywood's script-writers when creating cockney speech for the movies of the 1930s. It also prompted the authorities to look for clues to the identity of the writer which his spelling and use of certain words might reveal.

A second postcard sent to the Chairman of the Vigilance Committee rated particular attention.

> Say, Boss, you seem rare firghtened (sic). Guess I like to give you fits, but can't stop long enough to let you box of toys play copper games with me, but hope to see you when I don't hurry too much

> Goodbye Boss.

The use of slang such as 'quit', 'rare' 'frightened' and 'codding' led *The Times* to conclude that the writer was American. Other correspondents pointed out that 'codding' appeared in the *Oxford English Dictionary* and had been used for centuries as a low reference to hoax or joking. Shakespeare, said another, could scarcely have been accused of Americanism in his apparent preoccupation with cod-pieces. Another letter had mentioned 'buckled', and many observed that this was common London underworld slang for arrest. There was conjecture that 'box of toys' was a nautical term or simply cockney rhyming slang for 'boys'. The debate went on and on.

Jack didn't just taunt from the capital. A letter posted in Liverpool and received on 29 September, a day before the double murder, said:

> Beware. I shall be at work on the 1st and 2nd inst. in the Minories at twelve midnight, and I give the authorities a good chance but there is never a policeman near when I am at work.

This was followed by a note bearing the address: Prince William Street, Liverpool.

What fools the police are. I even gave them the name of the street where I am living.

From Glasgow Jack goaded:

> Think I'll quit using my nice sharp knife. Too good for whores. Have come here to buy a Scotch dirk. Ha! Ha! That will tickle up their ovaries.

Dr Thomas Dutton, a specialist in micro-photography, had made more than a hundred comparison microscopic slides of the letters. At least thirty-four of the notes were, in his opinion, written by the same hand.

Dutton claimed to have photographed the message scrawled on the wall in Goulston Street before it had been erased, but said that Sir Charles Warren had destroyed the prints which he had sent to the police.

Subsequent graphologists have pointed to the similarities of the 'From Hell' and the 'Old Boss' letters: sharp angles and dagger strokes apparently indicate extreme tension finding a vent in anger, and latent homosexuality was hinted at by loops beneath the line being returned on the wrong side of the letter.

In his memoirs, Dutton, for many years a leading figure in the Chichester and West Sussex Microscopic Society, judged the police as having paid too little attention to the letters. They had assumed that several hoaxers were at work and had ignored the fact that thirty-four were in the same hand, and these contained significant information.

Under the pen-name 'Nemo', a writer who had lived in India suggested that the mutilations indicated that they had been committed by a Malay, Lascar or other Asiatic.

> Unless caught red-handed [Nemo's phraseology was chillingly apt] such a man in ordinary life would be harmless enough, polite, not to say obsequious, in his manners and about the last a British policeman would suspect. But when the villain is primed with his opium, or bang, or gin, and inspired with his lust for slaughter and blood he would destroy his defenceless victim with the ferocity and cunning of the tiger; and past impunity and success would only have rendered him the more daring and reckless.

Somewhat less histrionically, Fred W. P. Jago of Plymouth wrote to *The Times* on 4 October:

> Sir. Another remarkable letter has been written by some bad fellow who signs himself 'Jack the Ripper'. The letter is said to be smeared with blood, and there is on it the print in blood of the

No. ~~52088.~~
57883

Criminal Investigation Department.

Gt. Scotland Yard,

23ʳᵈ July 188̸9

re Whitechapel Murders.

SIR,

I am directed by the Commissioner of Police of the Metropolis to acknowledge, with thanks, the receipt of your letter of the *20ᵗʰ inst*

I am, SIR,

Your obedient Servant,

R. ANDERSON,

Assistant Commissioner of Police.

The Commissioner of London Police

corrugated surface of a thumb. This may be that of a man or a woman.

It is inconceivable that a woman wrote or smeared such a letter, and therefore it may be accepted as a fact that the impression in blood is that of a man's thumb.

The surface of a thumb, so printed, is as clearly indicated as are the printed letters from any kind of type. Thus there is a possibility of identifying the blood-print on the letter with the thumb that made it, because the surface markings on no two thumbs are alike, and this a low-power microscope could reveal.

Mr Jago went on to suggest that tests be made to see if it was human blood and that the thumbs of suspects be compared with the print. Thumb size and class of hand would also need to be considered.

> All this the microscope could reveal. The print of a thumb would give as good evidence as that of a boot or shoe.

The suggestion in fact pre-dated the use of fingerprints by the police by more than a decade. In 1901 fingerprinting would be sanctioned in England and Wales. By 1905 the Metropolitan Police, who supervised the system, would have eighty thousand prints on record and would be adding about 350 slips weekly. In that year the first conviction would be obtained using the bloody fingerprint evidence found at a murder with robbery in Deptford, south London. But that was a generation away, and fingerprints played no part for Inspector Abberline and his men.

The apparent disinterest shown by the police may have sprung simply from the sheer volume of the correspondence. Sifting just over a score of similar-looking notes from thousands of letters was too mammoth a task to contemplate. Besides, the ill-spelled letter that had accompanied the kidney sent to Mr Lusk had been scrawled untidily, almost maniacally, whereas the 'Jack the Ripper' signatures were in the neat copperplate of an educated correspondent who had no spelling difficulties. But is it to be supposed that a maniacal killer under stress would write in the same style as in his calmer moments? The police thought so – but perhaps nobody had told Jack.

Just to compound the difficulties, Jack went on writing. Cards, simply addressed 'The Boss, Scotland Yard', would arrive with a pencilled annotation by alert postal sorters about time and place of posting.

That some of the boastful, exhibitionist letters were genuine there can be little doubt. For Jack, the ultimate exhibitionist, the letters are entirely in character. But it is not for his writing that Jack has gone down in history. Blood was Jack's ink. A flashing blade, his pen.

11

Person or Persons Unknown

THE *Illustrated Police News* of Saturday, 17 November carried two reports of some note on the same page.

PARDON OFFERED

The following notice was posted in Dorset Street and at all the police stations in the metropolis on Saturday:

'MURDER PARDON. Whereas, on November 8th or 9th in Miller's Court, Dorset Street, Spitalfields, Mary Jane Kelly was murdered by some person or persons unknown, the Secretary of State will advise the grant of Her Majesty's gracious Pardon to any accomplice, not being a person who contrived or actually committed the Murder, who shall give such information as shall lead to the discovery and conviction of the person or persons who committed the Murder.

> (Signed) Charles Warren
> The Commissioner of
> Police of the Metropolis
> Metropolitan Police Office
> 4, Whitehall Place.
> November 10th 1888

In the next column, under the insignificantly tiny headline 'Resignation of Sir Charles Warren', five lines heralded the exit of the commissioner. An MP speaking in parliament announced that his resignation had been tendered on the 8th and that it had been accepted.

Sir Charles, who had resisted all offers and pleas that a reward should be tendered had finally put his name to a remarkable inducement for information, and it had every appearance that he'd done so two days after he had left office.

Although he was leaving under a cloud, with public order a vexed issue and the maniacal killer still stalking the streets, Warren's career was by no means over. The history books show us that at the outbreak of the Boer War the old soldier, by now forty-eight, was back in uniform, commanding the Fifth Infantry Division. In the second attempt to raise the siege of Ladysmith he attacked the Boers. Spion Kop was captured and held for four days, but after severe fighting and heavy British losses, was evacuated. Unhappily, even here his blimpishness seems to have led him into conflict with his superiors. Lord Roberts subjected Warren's leadership to severe criticism.

Almost as soon as Mary Jane Kelly's body was discovered, rumours about a police cover-up began to circulate. By the time the inquest opened on Monday, 12 November, three days after the crime, as many unofficial questions were being asked on the streets as were being answered formally in the Shoreditch Town Hall. Even the venue for the inquest had raised a storm of protest, both in the press and from the reluctant jurors.

Why, it was asked, had the body been moved from the Spitalfields district to the Shoreditch mortuary? After all, the corpse had been found just two hundred yards from the scene of Annie Chapman's murder and only a few minute's walk from Berner Street, where Elizabeth Stride had been found. By moving the body to Shoreditch mortuary the inquest had been taken out of the control of Dr Wynne Baxter, who had been so critical of police methods when he had presided over the inquests on the earlier victims. His criticisms had not been well received at Scotland Yard, and the doctors had also resented his requirement that all the grisly facts should be revealed to the public.

In the Shoreditch coroner, Dr Roderick McDonald MP, the authorities certainly had a more amenable official. He ingeniously resisted the protests of local jurymen by citing that jurisdiction technically lay where the body lay, not where it was originally found, and managed to conclude the business after only a single day's testimony.

The morning after the inquest, the *Daily Telegraph* complained that comparatively little that was new had been elicited by the coroner's inquiry. The newspaper carefully reported details of a suspect.

Another Miller's Court prostitute, Mary Ann Cox, who lived at number five, had seen a man entering the court with Kelly on the fateful night. She had seen him clearly in the light of a street lamp directly opposite the doorway of number thirteen. He was short and stout, about thirty-six, dressed in a longish shabby coat and round billycock hat. She described his blotchy face and full, carroty moustache. He carried a tankard of ale.

The jury were reminded that the Hanbury Street victim had been seen with a dark, foreign-looking man, and a similar description was given of a suspect at the time of Polly Nichols' murder in Buck's Row.

Ten minutes before her body had been found in Mitre Square,

Catherine Eddowes had been seen with a man about thirty years old, with a fair complexion and fair moustache.

On the morning of the Hanbury Street murder a suspicious individual had been noticed in a local public house. He was of shabby-genteel appearance with a sandy moustache. The City police had been making enquiries without success for weeks past, and they did not believe that their suspect was the man described by Cox. However, the Metropolitan Police attached greater significance to her evidence.

Extraordinarily, the man Hutchinson, Kelly's acquaintance who had spoken to her in Commercial Street an hour or so before she was killed, was not called to give evidence. It wasn't until a few days later that newspapers began to report his description of the man seen with Kelly.

The conduct of the proceedings was not allowed to go entirely unquestioned, as is shown in this exchange between the coroner and a member of the jury being sworn in:

> 'I do not see why we should have the inquest thrown on our shoulders, when the murder did not happen in our district but in Whitechapel.'
>
> 'It did not happen in Whitechapel. Do you think we do not know what we are doing here, and that we do not know our own district? The jury are summoned in the ordinary way and they have no business to object. If they persist in their objection I shall know how to deal with them. Does any juror persist in objecting?'
>
> 'We are summoned for the Shoreditch district. This affair happened in Spitalfields.'
>
> 'It happened within my district.'
>
> 'This is not *my* district. I come from Whitechapel and Mr Baxter is my coroner.'

This was too much for the coroner, who stormed:

> 'I am not going to discuss the subject with jurymen at all. If any juryman says he distinctly objects, let him say so..'

He looked balefully over his spectacles before continuing:

> 'I may tell the jurymen that jurisdiction lies where the body lies, not where it was found, if there was doubt as to where the body was found.'

Dr McDonald's bombastic and unsympathetic stance is reflected in this exchange after a short adjournment later in the day:

> 'It has come to my ears that somebody has been making a statement to some of the jury as to their right and duty of being here. Has anyone during the interval spoken to the jury, saying that they should not be here today?'

Some jurymen shook their heads.

> 'Then I must have been misinformed. I should have taken good
> care that he would have had a quiet life for the rest of the week if
> anybody had interfered with my jury.'

The jurors viewed the body, then went to Miller's Court, after which
they returned to the town hall to begin the hearing.

Formal evidence of identification was given by Joseph Barnett,
described by the *Star* as 'a fish porter of six and twenty years old, and
looking very respectable for one of his class'. He stated that he had lived
with Mary for one year and eight months. The ordeal of this poor man,
who had to fight with a stutter while tearfully presenting his grim
evidence, shows through clearly in the newspaper reports of the time,
even though they conflict in detail. The reporter from the *Daily
Telegraph* wrote:

> 'I have seen the body, and I identify it by the ear and eyes which is
> all that I recognize.'

The *Illustrated Police News* substituted 'hair' for 'ear' which is probably
more likely.

Barnett told how Mary had been born in Limerick and had moved to
Wales at an early age. She had six brothers and sisters, one brother was
in the army. At sixteen she had married a collier who had died in an
explosion. Mary had gone to Cardiff to live with her cousin, where her
street-walking began. Life in a fashionable house in the West End
followed, and then apparently there was some foray into the French
capital, but details were sparse. On her return to England she had lived
in Ratcliffe Highway and had remained in the East End ever since.

The Divisional Police Surgeon Mr George Bagster-Phillips, who had
attended other victims, deposed that he had arrived at the scene at 11.15
a.m. He had looked through the window and, hardly surprisingly, had
been satisfied that the mutilated corpse was not in need of his immediate
professional assistance. He had remained outside the room until 1.30
p.m. when the door had been forced open by McCarthy, under the
direction of Superintendent T. Arnold of H Division.

Bagster-Phillips concluded that the severance of the right carotid
artery, inflicted while the victim was lying at the right hand side of her
bedstead, had been the immediate cause of death.

The body had been placed in a plain coffin and removed to
Shoreditch mortuary shortly before four o'clock, in a horse-drawn
spring van followed by a crowd of onlookers.

Inspector Abberline explained why there had been a delay of two and a half hours between finding the body and breaking down the door. Inspector Beck of H Division, who was in charge of Leman Street police station, had been summoned by McCarthy's man and, having arrived at the scene, had established a blockade of Miller's Court, refusing to let anyone in or out until bloodhounds were put on the trail of the murderer. It was feared that the scent would be seriously interfered with if indiscriminate traffic were allowed. The bloodhounds were asked for immediately, but could not be found.

There had in fact been no trained bloodhounds in London at any time during the preceding fortnight. Following the earlier trials, arrangements had been made for the animals to go to the scene-of-crime in the event of another murder occurring. However, Mr Brough, their owner, had returned to Scarborough and left the dogs in the care of a friend, Mr Taunton, pending their sale to the police. Sir Charles Warren wouldn't give any guarantee of purchase, so Brough demanded the return of his dogs. Bhurgo was sent to a show in Brighton, while the other hound remained with Taunton.

Shortly afterwards Taunton received a police telegram asking for his assistance in tracking burglars in Commercial Street. Taunton pointed out that as the police themselves had destroyed any scent, the hounds would accomplish nothing. Brough, their owner, had no guarantee of compensation and feared that the dogs might be poisoned. He recalled both dogs to Scarborough immediately.

Taunton thought the police naive, and his views were reported in the *Daily Telegraph*:

> It was then broad daylight and the streets crowded with people. The only chance for the hounds would be in the event of a murdered body being discovered, as the others were, in the small hours of the morning, and the dogs being put on the trail before many people were about.

But all this background, this abortive negotiation for the purchase of the dogs, was unknown to the officers of H Division, who stood around outside the locked door of number thirteen, waiting for the hounds that never came. Eventually Superintendent Arnold arrived and said that the order about the dogs had been countermanded and that the door must now be forced.

Sir Melville Macnaghten, the astute Commissioner whose legendary notes on the crimes give historians important clues. For years, as a reminder of the unsolved crimes, he kept on his desk a photograph of the mutilated remains of Mary Kelly.

Abberline's evidence included his investigation of the fireplace at Miller's Court. There were traces of a large fire having been kept up in the grate. It had been so hot it had melted the spout of the kettle. The ashes contained a portion of a brim of a hat and a skirt and it seemed as if a large quantity of women's clothing had been burnt. The Inspector suggested that the fire had been made to give the sadist light for his ghastly task; there was, however, a candle in a broken wine glass on the table which could have served that purpose. Could there have been another, more sinister reason for the fire?

It is generally acknowledged that with the murder of Mary Kelly the killer had achieved the ultimate in his perverted goals. In this murder, the only one to take place indoors, Jack had killed and mutilated his victim and then removed a foetus. The foetus was never found, which suggests that perhaps one dreadful final act had taken place. *Had the unborn child been cooked and eaten?*

A procession of drabs occupying rooms at McCarthy's Rents appeared and spoke of knowing Mary. A few had seen her, slightly drunk, in the hours up to 2.15 a.m., when the roofless Hutchinson had seen her go into number thirteen with the stranger. Sarah Lewis, a laundress, said she had heard a cry of 'Murder!' at about 3.30 a.m. The same cry had been heard by another Dorset Street prostitute, Elizabeth Prater, who lived in the room above Mary's. Despite Rippermania, both witnesses had found this cry quite unremarkable in Dorset Street and had gone back to sleep.

The wife of a lodging-house deputy, Caroline Maxwell, caused a minor stir when she claimed to have seen Mary Kelly standing in the court for half an hour from eight on the morning of the crime, hours after the official time of her death. She said she had spoken to Kelly, who had told her she was feeling unwell and had pointed to some vomit in the road which was, she said, the remains of a glass of beer. Mrs Maxwell lived at 14, Dorset Street and had known Mary for about four months. Her evidence was given firmly and convincingly:

> 'I'm sure it was the deceased. I'm willing to swear it.'
> 'You *are* sworn', growled the coroner.

Kelly may well have been experiencing morning sickness at that time, which beer from the Britannia would have done little to ameliorate. The detail embellishing Mrs Maxwell's evidence suggests that the events really happened, but the recollections were probably from another day. Inspector Abberline always refused to accept that it was a mistake. Either she was lying or it was true. It was a disparity that might have

been cleared up by longer cross-examination that could have exposed flaws, but that was never to take place.

At all events the testimony of the medical men was at odds with the lodging-house deputy's wife.

Dr Thomas Bond, a leading lecturer in forensic medicine, consultant to the police and author of several medical publications, described that the onset of rigor mortis had already begun when he examined the body at 2.00 p.m. Six to twelve hours can elapse before rigidity sets in. The body had been almost cold at two o'clock and the remains of a meal found in what was left of her stomach was partly digested. Indications were that Mary had breathed her last not long after 2.00 a.m.

The comparatively new science of forensic photography was called upon, and scene-of-crime photographs were admitted in evidence. One photograph referred to by Sir Melville Macnaghten in his confidential notes now known as the Macnaghten Papers, is of particular interest:

> The last murder (Kelly) is the only one that took place in a room and the murderer must have been at least two hours engaged. A photo was taken of the woman, as she was found lying on the bed, without seeing which it is impossible to imagine the awful mutilation.

A curious fact is that the photograph, like all the surviving photographs of Ripper victims, was taken by the City of London Police, despite the fact that Miller's Court was in Metropolitan territory.

Sir Charles Warren had ordered that no entry be made before the bloodhounds had been to a scene-of-crime. An interesting theory proposed by Donald Rumbelow is that, although the order was observed by the Met., the men of the City Police had ignored it. It seems that as the morning had passed and the Metropolitan Police seemed to be doing nothing, somebody had asked the City Police to help. When they attended, their justification for entering the room was to photograph the body. They probably entered by the window. It was said that at 1.30 p.m. Superintendent Arnold had decided that they could not wait for Warren, and had one of the windows removed.

Later, the curious ritual of photographing the victim's eyes had been carried out. There was a theory that was to last well into the first quarter of the twentieth century that in cases of violent death the last images were fixed permanently to the retina of the eye. A photograph taken when the eye had been drawn a little way out of the socket could thus, it was believed, identify the killer.

It was nonsense of course, but it was a superstition that reached right into our own century when, forty years later, the body of the Essex constable PC Gutteridge was found on the Romford–Ongar road. The village constable's notebook and helmet were beside him and in his hand was a pencil with which he had obviously been about to write. He had died without a struggle, struck in the head by two bullets at fairly close range. Both eyes had then been very deliberately destroyed by two further shots.

If Dr Roderick McDonald, in his role as coroner, had upset the jury by his strictures, he was to upset the press and public even more. After less than half a day, he closed the inquest at 4.30 p.m., with the following announcement to the court:

> There is evidence which I do not propose to call. For if we at once make public every fact brought forward in connection with this terrible murder the ends of justice might be retarded.

He was successful in admitting only a very perfunctory part of Dr Phillips' evidence, which he promised would be heard in full at a future date. At this time, only just enough to allow the jury to find a cause of death was allowed. The Coroner was of the opinion that if the jury adjourned for further evidence it would only cause yet more expense and trouble. It was quite sufficient if they could come to a decision as to cause of death.

The foreman of the jury consulted his colleagues, doubtless happy to escape details of the post-mortem, and decided that they had enough evidence. The not unexpected verdict was returned. Murder by person or persons unknown.

The press was outraged. The murder that had provided more clues than any of the preceding four cried out for the opportunity to cross-examine witnesses – particularly the woman who claimed to have seen Kelly at 8.00 a.m. on Friday. The *Daily Telegraph* called on the Home Secretary for a new inquest, but it was not to be.

In the space of two and a half hours in the squalid little room, the maniacal killer had worked tirelessly. Jack had done his best to do his worst. He had piled horror upon horror, each obscenity taking him further in the annals of abomination than any single crime before, or perhaps since. That is possibly the reason why when, lit like some demon in the flickering red firelight, Jack straightened up, wiped his hands, and stepped into the courtyard, it marked the end of a reign of terror and the start of a century of conjecture.

A void opened up which, try as they might, neither the authorities nor a succession of investigators have filled. It is as if the moment Jack stepped out of number thirteen, he ceased to exist.

Murder of Mary Kelly: description of main suspects

The Murderer Described:
Mary Ann Cox, a wretched-looking specimen of East End womanhood said; 'I live at room number five, Miller's Court. I am a widow, and having been unfortunate lately, I have to get my living on the streets. On Thursday night at quarter to twelve, I saw the deceased, much intoxicated in Dorset Street. There was with her a short, stout man, shabbily dressed. He had a longish dark coat on, not an overcoat, and he had a pot of ale in his hand. He had a round felt hat on. He wore a full carroty moustache and had a blotchy face, a clean-shaven chin and very slight whiskers.'

(The Star, Monday, 12 November)

Well-dressed man, thirty-four to thirty-five years old, 5 ft 6 in, pale complexion, dark hair, slight moustache, curled up at each end. Long, dark coat, collar and cuffs trimmed with astrakhan, dark-coloured jacket underneath. Light-coloured waistcoat, dark trousers, button boots and gaiters with white buttons. White shirt, black tie, gold horseshoe pin. Jewish appearance and respectable. Gold watch-chain, big seal and red stone. Parcel in left hand, with strap around it.

(Witness Hutchinson)

12

Reflections of the Ripper

IT WAS TO BE A FEW YEARS before it was certain that Jack had finished, for whatever reason, his reign of terror. Each time another prostitute met a violent end his name would be invoked.

A seven-page memorandum in the Home Office Ripper file has already been mentioned. This was handwritten by Sir Melville Macnaghten, who became head of CID in 1903. Known as the Macnaghten Papers, the memorandum was written to disprove a newspaper story about a man who had been running around the East End stabbing ladies' bottoms with a pair of nail-scissors. For some obscure reason, police and others believed that this established that the culprit, Thomas Cutbush, a deranged syphilitic fetishist, was Jack the Ripper. In the memorandum, Macnaghten wrote:

> Now the Whitechapel murderer had five victims, and five victims only.
> Nichols; Chapman; Stride; Eddowes; Kelly.

But there were those who believed that other murders bore the mark of the Ripper. The slayings of Emma Smith, in April 1888 and Martha Tabram four months later, had been attributed to Jack. In June 1889, seven months after Kelly's death, the newspaper headlines were clamouring about a headless body found in the Thames. Subsequently identified from scars, the torso had belonged to Elizabeth Jackson, a prostitute from Sloane Square. The following month, a Whitechapel street-walker named Alice MacKenzie was found with her throat slit. She had also been disembowelled.

The last name in this grim catalogue of possible additions to the certain five is Frances Coles, a twenty-five-year-old prostitute who had been found dying of abdominal injuries. Her throat had also been cut. She was found beneath the arches of the Great Eastern Railway Company at Swallow Gardens, Orman Street, Whitechapel, by a patrolling policeman. That she was still alive when Constable Thompson found her, was attributed to his interruption of the killer. Thompson had seen a man fleeing from the gardens.

Six months passed, and early in 1965 Aniuta Kaliniak, a pretty sixteen-year-old was found dead in the basement of a leather factory near her home in an eastern part of Warsaw. A large spike had been driven into her vagina. She had been raped and mutilated.

When the body of Janka Popieleski was found at Poznan on All Saints Day in November that year, the injuries and mutilations were such that the authorities suppressed all details. With each new corpse the murderer's frenzy had increased. This was a mobile Ripper, who had taken a long screwdriver 140 miles west from his previous victim to perform ghastly outrages on the young hotel receptionist. While police put up road blocks in search of the heavily-bloodstained murderer, another letter arrived.

> Only tears of sorrow can wash out the stain of shame, only pangs of suffering can blot out the fires of lust.

Six months later on the 1966 May Day national holiday the disembowelled body of Marysia Galazka was found by her father in the garden of their home. The seventeen-year-old had gone out for just a few moments to look for her cat.

Time was running out for the Polish Ripper. Unlike his nineteenth-century counterpart he wouldn't, perhaps couldn't, stop killing.

When the mutilated remains of a girl was found in the Cracow to Warsaw express on Christmas Eve 1966, the links that had been so long denied to the authorities began to snap into place. The victim was Janina Kozielska of Cracow. She had been strangled and her abdomen and thighs mercilessly ripped apart and strewn around the carriage. She was a part-time model at the bona fide Art Lovers Club, where amateur painters met. The latest of the Red Spider's letters had been found in the mail box on the train. The red ink, a mixture of red artist paint and turpentine, was suddenly the all-important link.

A member of the club who had painted pictures of women with mutilated stomachs was arrested. Lucien Staniak, a twenty-six-year-old publisher's translator, confessed to twenty murders, and police learned that his nightmare pursuit had started when his parents and sister had been run down by a car driven by a woman driver. The woman had not been punished, and in some warped way this had set Staniak on his trail of terror.

Staniak was sentenced to death for six of the murders, but was later sent to the asylum at Katowice.

Fate had been merciless to the Kosielska family, for Janina's sister had been murdered in Warsaw in 1964, but this fact was an important link in the chain. By painstakingly checking railway tickets and reservations, and by admirable following-up of clues, the police found their way to the heart of the Red Spider's web. It had taken only thirty-one days from the finding of Janina's body in the train to the capture of Staniak. But for one eighteen-year-old student from the Lodz Institute of Cinematic Art, Bozhena Raczkiewicz, whose mutilated and ravaged body was found in a railway station that morning, it had been just one day too long.

In Boston in June 1962, Albert DeSalvo began to carve a bloody, thirteen-bodied, trail of sickening sadism. It was almost eighteen months before he was captured.

Ten years later, in a Yorkshire village, an amiable-looking young lorry-driver, Peter Sutcliffe, was contemplating the first of his thirteen victims, not all prostitutes, whose killings led him to be dubbed 'The Yorkshire Ripper'.

Unlike Jack of eighty-four years previously, Sutcliffe stalked by car, picking up women, killing them with hammer blows and then subjecting them to frenzied stabbing and slashing with a knife and screwdriver. In only one case was a victim raped – the killer seemed to need only the savagery for his satisfaction.

Sutcliffe's eventual capture was more the outcome of luck than astute policing, and the hunt for him had curious parallels with that of his famous predecessor. The police had been taunted with letters and even tape-recordings, and, as in 1888, public frustration with police impotence had resulted in changes in senior ranks. Like their Victorian counterparts' reporting of ineptitudes, the newspapers headlined the fact that the police had let Sutcliffe go nine times during their £4,000,000 manhunt.

At the age of thirty-four, Sutcliffe began a life sentence from which, we are told, it is unlikely he will ever be released.

13

Identity Parade

HUNT THE RIPPER IS A GAME that knows no boundaries. Its origins began in the courts and tenements of Whitechapel, in the columns of penny-illustrateds, then spread to the club-rooms of Pall Mall and even, although with little success, to Scotland Yard itself. It is an endless pursuit and has accused all strata of society from the highest to the humble, from royalty to ragamuffin.

At the time, the authorities looked at the following general description of suspects:

> Man twenty-eight. 5 ft 8 in. Dark complexion. Small dark moustache. Dress – black diagonal coat, collar and tie, hard felt hat, respectable appearance, carried a parcel wrapped in newspaper.
>
> Man thirty. 5 ft 5 in. Fair, hair dark, small brown moustache. Dress – dark jacket and trousers, black cap with peak.
>
> (Stride murder)
>
> Someone residing in the immediate neighbourhood. (Later revised.) Man. Age thirty. 5 ft 7 or 8 in, fair, fair moustache, medium build. Dress – pepper and salt colour loose jacket, cloth cap with peak of same material, reddish kerchief tied in knot. Appearance of sailor.
>
> (Eddowes murder)

Discounting the sailor's scarf and the subjective comments about nautical appearance, these descriptions could be of the same man. Allowing for witnesses' fallibility and the ill-lit conditions of these night-time sightings, the authorities appeared to have a clear idea of their quarry.

The police clearly believed that after performing the deed the killer would be muddy and bloodstained, but several authorities have observed that this premise assumes two things. Firstly, that the victim would be lying on the ground, either voluntarily or by force, and secondly that blood from the carotid artery in the throat would have to gush some three feet in order to saturate the killer, who would be standing above or in front of the victim.

The state of Whitechapel alleys and backyards on damp autumn nights hardly invited even the drabbest of creatures to lie down on the cobbles. It is far more likely that Polly, Annie, Liz and Kate, like other unfortunates, would service their clients while leaning against the wall, either with their backs against it, or (having regard for common contraception precautions), bending forward against the wall.

A glance at female clothing of the period shows that if a victim placed herself facing the wall, with her voluminous skirts raised above her back, the murderer behind her would be in an excellent position to slit her throat from behind, and still be protected from the initial surge of gore.

The early statement by the authorities that 'someone residing in the immediate vicinity be sought', was amended, and the net was cast wider.

A hundred years on, making a certain decision about the culprit's identity is as difficult as ever. Like a child faced with a chocolate-box selection at Christmas, first one choice is made, then discarded, to be followed by another, and yet another. The Ripper selection of chocolate-coated candy is the biggest yet. Some are gold-wrapped and have been found by many investigators to be more attractive than others. But one man's fancy is another's fiction, and by now the gold-wrapping is frequently tarnished.

So we too, as many others have done before us, begin the process of sifting through the suspects. Our selection will not be exhaustive, for such a list could never be compiled. There will always be new suspects, silver-wrapped, gold-wrapped, and flavour of the month. But for now, lift the lid and make your choice.

DRUITT, *Montague John*

b 15 August 1857
d ? December 1888

The body was floating, half-submerged, strands of green river weed clinging to what was left of the battered face. It was obvious to waterman Winslow that his grim find at Thornycroft's Reach, Chiswick, had entered the river at least a month previously.

The stones which had initially taken the body to the gravelly bottom of the Thames had eventually proved insufficient, for the corpse, bloated with gaseous putrefaction, had returned to the surface.

The mortuary was close by, and there a closer examination yielded the sort of bits and pieces that are always carried around in pockets, but which only become significant when sifted as clues to identity. There was not a great deal of money, just £2.17.2d. In addition, a silver watch on a gold chain with a guinea attached, a pair of gloves and a white handkerchief. As well as these, there was the unused portion of a railway ticket from Charing Cross to Hammersmith, which lay only a mile downstream from Thornycroft's torpedo works and could well have been the place where the young man had entered the water, in this tidal stretch of the Thames. The ticket was dated 1 December, a month before.

The sodden remains of two cheques, drawn on the London Provincial Bank for £50 and £16, and a railway season ticket from Blackheath to London gave the authorities their first clue to the identity of the well-dressed man. A telegram was sent to Bournemouth.

Two days later, the inquest at the Lamb and Tap in Chiswick revealed more about the deceased. The body was that of Montague John Druitt. The son of well-to-do parents, his father was a leading surgeon in Wimborne, Dorset. The practice of medicine ran in the family: Montague's uncle Robert and cousin Lionel were both doctors. Montague had spent six years at Winchester and had then won a scholarship to New College, Oxford. Though popular, his academic career was undistinguished. He scraped through his second-class honours degree in Classical Moderation (1878) and managed a third-class Classics. He graduated in 1880. Three years later he had the customary privilege of purchasing his MA.

Although he was academically weak, descriptions of his years at prep school and university reveal a successful and outgoing personality. His competence at sports is reflected in his prowess at fives (he was school champion in 1875), and he played first-eleven cricket at Lords the following year.

The two years following Montague's graduation are somewhat shrouded. Did he consider the family career of medicine? Certainly there seems to have been some delay in his decision to follow law, for he did not apply for admission to the Inner Temple until May 1882. He was borrowing heavily to pay the fees, and, probably for the same reason, he became a teacher at a crammers school for forty boys in Blackheath, some forty-five minutes on the railway from London.

Montague was called to the Bar in April 1885 and shortly afterwards his father died of a heart attack, leaving an estate of almost £17,000. Most of it was shared among his three daughters, and the eldest son,

William, inherited a farm. The remaining three sons – including Montague – got very little.

In shared chambers at 9, King's Bench Walk, Montague joined the Western Circuit and Winchester Sessions as a barrister.

Even with a legacy it would have been difficult to make a success in this overcrowded profession. No record exists of the fledgling barrister even getting a brief. He was to continue as master at Mr Valentine's School at Eliot Place, Blackheath, until the winter of 1888, when he was dismissed abruptly. Rumour had it that homosexual practices with the boys had led to this speedy exit. But much more sinister is the undoubted evidence that at this time the successful all-rounder, the once-popular, sports-loving, outgoing Montague, had undergone a considerable personality change.

His mother Anne, aged fifty-eight, was confined in a private mental home in Chiswick. She would die there on 15 December 1890 of melancholia and brain disease. After visiting his mother, Montague believed that he too was going mad. A note suggesting suicide was found:

> Since Friday I felt I was going to be like Mother and the best thing for me was to die.

On 11 December, word reached his brother William, a Bournemouth solicitor, that Montague had not been seen at his chambers since the 3rd. His brother was concerned enough to visit London and the Blackheath school, where William found the note addressed to him.

Few theorists believe that the Ripper was a doctor. However it is difficult to argue with those who see some anatomical expertise with the butcher's knife. The police suspected that a post-mortem knife was used by the murderer, and certainly Montague would have had no difficulty in obtaining one of these. Cousin Lionel's surgery at the Minories was but half a mile away from Whitechapel. The King's Bench Walk chambers were within twenty minutes walk.

It cannot be denied that many leading investigators at the time considered that Druitt was the Ripper. The address of his cousin's surgery is a tempting link with the East End. Testimony to his physical strength is borne out by his sporting prowess, and ambidexterity is confirmed by his success at fives, played with two hands instead of a bat.

A contemporary photograph shows only a clean-shaven Druitt, but it was taken at Winchester a dozen or more years before the crimes.

After the murder of Mary Kelly, the police expected more crimes in November. When three months passed without further incident, patrols

Montague Druitt. Was he the suspect referred to in Macnaghten's cryptic comment that his greatest regret was that he had 'become a detective officer six months after Jack the Ripper committed suicide'?

were reduced. The authorities seemed to lose interest in the case and in March 1889 asked that the specially set up Whitechapel Vigilance Committee be disbanded. The public alarm at this prompted Albert Backert, a prominent member of the Committee, to approach senior police officers.

Backert's complaints of complacency were met with a request that he be sworn to secrecy on the understanding that he be given certain information. Cryptically he was told; 'The Ripper is dead. Fished out of the Thames two months ago. It would only cause pain to relatives if more was said.'

Backert was not a happy man. Years later he said he had never believed the tale. Another figure who held the story in contempt was Detective Inspector Abberline, who was quite certain that the Ripper was alive and free.

Sir Melville Macnaghten said of one suspect (without naming him):

> I have always held strong opinions regarding him, and the more I think the matter over, the stronger do the opinions become. The truth, however, will never be known, and did indeed, at one time lie at the bottom of the Thames, if my conjections be correct!

Druitt was one of three possible suspects mentioned in Macnaghten's notes.

Druitt's movements in the months of the Whitechapel murders are better-documented than many. Following a year in which he had taken all ten of the first innings wickets at an important Surrey match in Kingston, many fixture lists include the name of the keen cricketer. Twenty-four hours after the Nichols slaying, Druitt was batting at Wimborne, Dorset. He was playing at Blackheath only five hours after the Chapman murder. But these are far from cast-iron alibis.

Does the fiend of Whitechapel sleep under a stone cross in Wimborne cemetery? One of the most popular suspects among many police officials, Druitt had the opportunity and certainly seemed to suffer a sinister personality change during the autumn of the murders. However, he had no criminal background and some would consider that he was simply a dreadfully despondent young man, fearful that he was going insane. Whitechapel fiend, or Whitehall scapegoat?

CHAPMAN, *George*

(Severin Antoniovich Klosowski)

b 14 December 1865   Eyes: blue
d 7 April 1903   Nose/mouth: medium
Height: medium   Chin/face: longish
Hair: dark

Chapman or Klosowski, to use his real name, has always been a strong suspect. His background, his opportunity, his criminality – all match. Only his known *modus operandi* makes the jigsaw an uncomfortable fit and, for many, discounts his involvement in the crimes.

A one-time medical student, he was granted the degree of junior

surgeon in December by the Polish government in Warsaw, and served in the Russian Army as a surgeon's assistant. He emigrated to London in 1888, and under the name of Ludwig Klosowski became a Whitechapel hairdresser, living near to where the Ripper murders took place. He is said to have had a barber shop in the basement of George Yard Buildings in August 1888, when Emma Smith was murdered.

Physically, Klosowski resembled the scant descriptions of the murderer. His use of American slang is significant when considering the colloquialisms used in the Ripper letters.

Klosowski's marriage to Lucy Baderski was probably bigamous – there was certainly talk of a previous marriage in Poland. During the next year they lived at a number of Whitechapel addresses and then went to Jersey City, USA. However, Mrs Klosowski soon returned alone, because of her husband's involvement with another woman. Klosowski returned from America in 1892 and was reunited with Lucy. Again they lived in the East End, but the philandering dandy, trying harder and harder to appear English, soon deserted her and their two children once again.

He took up with another woman, Annie Chapman (not to be confused with the Ripper victim), and adopted her surname. For some reason she became frightened of him and left him after a year.

By 1895, Chapman had set up house with a married woman, Mary Spinks, using her money to open a barber shop in Hastings. His 'wife' played the piano to accompany his 'musical shaves'.

But Chapman was a shiftless character, and within six months he and Mrs Spinks were back in London. He embarked on a new career as tavern-keeper at the Prince of Wales, Bartholomew Square, off the City Road. It was here on Christmas Day, 1897, that Mrs Spinks died, apparently of consumption.

Chapman moved to the Grapes at Bishop Stortford, and later back to London, where he was landlord of the Monument in Union Street, the Borough. His final tenancy, the Crown, also in Union Street, was where the police finally caught up with him. But not until two more 'wives' had died.

The bodies of Mrs Spinks and Chapman's two other 'wives' were secretly exhumed, and the police were astonished by their remarkable state of preservation. Experts were not surprised to find that the poison antimony had been administered and was the cause of all three women's deaths. Chapman's biggest blunder had been to choose a poison with these remarkable preservative effects. On 25 October 1902 he was arrested and charged with murder.

He was tried at the Central Criminal Court before Mr Justice Grantham. In contrast to the four days' duration of the trial, the jury needed only eleven minutes for their deliberation. 'The Borough Poisoner' was executed on 7 April 1903.

It is worth noting that during Chapman's two years in New Jersey, several Ripper-like murders took place there. These ceased early in 1892 when Chapman returned to London. New York police conferred with the Yard, but Chapman had disappeared.

Chief Inspector Abberline had spotted Chapman in a Whitechapel shop and had been struck by the Pole's resemblance to a man arrested after the second murder, but who had been released, proved innocent. The Inspector remained convinced that Chapman was the Ripper but was never able to find enough evidence to pin the crimes on him. In later years he cited what evidence there was against Chapman: his bloodletting background; his physical resemblance to Ripper descriptions; and the claim by Lucy Baderski of overnight absences at relevant times.

But is it likely that Jack the Ripper, so steeped in blood, would find his 'jolly' in coldly administering poison? Perhaps this is the strongest argument against Chapman's culpability.

CLARENCE, HRH Prince Albert Victor, Duke of

b 8 January 1864
d 14 January 1892

> A thin young man, slightly taller than his brother and sister, brown, wavy hair, receding. Oval face, aquiline nose, large gentle doe-like eyes, buoyant cavalry moustache, waxed and turned up at ends.
>
> (Contemporary description)

His Royal Highness Prince Albert Victor, Duke of Clarence and Avondale, grandson of Queen Victoria and eldest son of the future King Edward VII, would eventually have come to the throne of England. In the event, his death – recorded as being from pneumonia – left the succession to his younger brother, who became King George V in 1911.

The theory that Eddy (his nickname) was the Ripper, broke upon a startled world press in 1970. Dr Thomas Stowell, a retired surgeon, made public the results of a research he had made forty years before. An exclusive examination of the private papers of Sir William Gull,

Eddy, Duke of Clarence. As much an enigma in his own time as in ours, lacking the Saxe-Coburg charisma of his father, who disliked him and thought him a dunce and unfit to be king. His death is still shrouded in mystery. Was he killer or victim?

Physician Extraordinary to Queen Victoria, had, he said, pointed the finger unmistakably at the Prince.

The story caused world-wide reaction. Newspapers carried it in every language and there was considerable debate. The old surgeon Stowell died shortly after the story broke, and his family destroyed all his papers.

History books tell us that Eddy succumbed to the great European 'flu epidemic of 1892, but Stowell insisted that the Prince died of syphilitic softening of the brain in a private mental home near Sandringham, claiming that Gull had written so in his notes.

Frank Spiering, sometime private-eye and American author of *Prince Jack*, published in 1978, offered an audacious challenge to the Queen when he asked her to open her files on her great-uncle. He dared her 'to tell what you know about his acts of murder and his own extraordinary death'. Her Majesty declined with much greater grace than the challenger deserved.

Spiering's claim that Eddy had admitted the Whitechapel Murders while being treated under hypnosis, went unanswered. So, too, the claim that the Duke's death in 1892 resulted from a morphine overdose, arranged by Buckingham Palace as a means of removing a 'deranged killer from the Royal Family'.

Let us return to Dr Stowell's revelations in 1970, stemming from his researches into the Royal Surgeon's private papers.

Sir William Gull's notes had traced the downward path of Eddy from an early age. In 1879, Victoria's far-flung Empire reached around the globe. Eddy embarked on a three-year world tour with his younger brother George (later George V). Their ship, HMS Bacchante, called at Australia, and Stowell believes that the young Duke was there seduced and contracted the syphilis that was to kill him aged twenty-eight.

The surgeon surmised that an acute attack of typhoid together with his youthfulness left the Duke poorly equipped to resist the four-stage disease of syphilis. The symptoms exhibited by his grandfather, a manic-depressive, had perhaps also been inherited.

Eddy seems to have been popular with the people. It wasn't just the East Enders who affectionately called him 'collar and cuffs', a nickname which his father, the Prince of Wales, delighted in using. Eddy's neck was astonishingly long – 'like a swan', was how one Royal described it. When not in uniform he would wear an unusually high starched collar. It was said that 'dear', 'good', and 'kind' was how his relatives described him. He was also quite uneducated and listless and apparently caused Queen Victoria great concern as she viewed his prospects as future king.

On his return to England, the pleasure-seeking Duke was found in a Cleveland Street brothel during a police raid. Next morning the newspapers boldly carried references to 'Arrest of the highest in the land'. The brothel, doubtless with the laudable intention of being all things to all men, catered both for homosexual and heterosexual clients.

As a result of the raid, Eddy's personal equerry was forced to flee the country and a scandal ensued. Among the unanswered questions was one about gold pencils being given to telegraph boys. This occurred in the mid-1880s, and Queen Victoria was most decidedly not amused. Before the question about the gold pencils could be resolved, Eddy had been packed off to sea again.

The grisly killings which Stowell laid at the door of Prince Eddy were claimed to be in retaliation for syphilis contracted during homosexual activities. (Though it must be said that all the evidence that Eddy was a homosexual seems circumstantial.) The murders began, thought Stowell, as Eddy's infected brain began to crumble.

Would the educationally sub-normal Prince have had the elementary surgical knowledge required for the speed and certainty with which the viscera were removed? Perhaps not, though the training royalty received in dissecting venison in the field might establish some precedent.

According to Stowell, Gull's papers showed that with their worst fears confirmed by the Kelly murder, the Royal Family had the Prince committed to a private asylum near Ascot. Such was the success of his treatment there that he was released very quickly and was able to accompany his parents on a five-month cruise in 1889. The *Graphic Magazine* published the following itinerary:

May	1889	Duke opens dock. Belfast
9 November	1889	Commenced tour of India. Returned May 1890.
June	1890	Opened new Gardens and promenade. Scarborough.
23 June	1890	Took seat in House of Lords.
4 January	1892	Attended funeral of Prince Victor of Hohenlohe.

It was at this funeral, in a wintry, gusty London, that Prince Eddy was said to have caught a cold. The capital was in the grip of a thick yellow fog which had descended at Christmas and lasted into the New Year. The family party to celebrate the impending birthday of the Prince assembled at Sandringham but was decimated by illness, influenza, colds, and even typhoid, from which Prince George was recovering. It was into this gathering (if official accounts are to be believed) that Eddy came, following the funeral.

On 7 January, the day before his birthday, Eddy felt unwell while out shooting. He took to his bed and his condition worsened. Eddy had been unable to attend his birthday dinner. That his family had no idea of just how serious his condition was is seen in the telegram sent by his mother, the Princess of Wales, to Queen Victoria, two hundred miles away at Osborne. 'Thanks so much for kind wishes. Poor Eddy got influenza, cannot dine, so tiresome.'

Within a week it was over. At 9.35 a.m. 14 January 1892, Prince Albert Victor, heir-presumptive to the throne of England, lay dead.

And that was all the world knew until the new version of Prince Eddy's death was published by Stowell in 1970.

Colin Wilson recalls an article on Jack the Ripper by Dr Harold Dearden. The doctor re-told an incident in the trenches in the Somme in 1918. A brother officer was celebrating his fortieth birthday. At this makeshift party he told how his father ran a mental home near London. As a boy of ten, the officer had had a visit to a pantomime cancelled because of the admission of a violent and noisy patient, one of his father's oldest friends. The boy was convinced that the patient was Jack the Ripper. Could this have been the mental home that the Royal Surgeon had mentioned in his notes? Some years before reading this, and long before the Stowell story of the Duke of Clarence, Wilson had received an anonymous letter from a woman who said that Jack the Ripper had died in her father's nursing home near Ascot. The soldier's sister?, wondered Wilson.

Eddy, Duke of Clarence, is an enigma. On the one hand he is probably the most public of candidates, but on the other hand he had a private life that is even more shadowy now than it was a century ago.

In his biography, *Clarence*, Michael Harrison laments:

> The destruction of Eddy's correspondence, and discreet silence maintained about his private activities have made the task of assessing his character no easy one.

At his bedside was his fiancée, Princess May of Teck, who would marry his brother George and become Queen Mary. Stowell would have us believe that the young prince engaged to the lovely princess was also the patient of whom Sir William Gull wrote: 'Informed Blank that his son was dying of syphilis of the brain'. Stowell left little doubt that Sir William's 'Blank' referred to Eddy's father, the Prince of Wales.

Was Eddy really suffering from brain decay and some inherited melancholic condition? Or was a limp and languid young man cruelly cheated of his birthright by succumbing to a 'flu epidemic, his memory to be tarnished eighty years later by the revelations of a dying man?

GULL, Sir William Withy

(with John Netley and another)

b 1816
d 29 January 1890

Arguably the most remarkable of the suspects might be the trio named above. Surely this candidature ranks equal to that of the Duke of Clarence, and by curious coincidence the web woven by the three also encompasses Eddy.

If this is the murder 'team', then their activities involve an astonishing catalogue of intrigue, death lists, conspiracy by leading Freemasons, kidnapping, and a government cover-up on a monumental scale.

In August 1973, Joseph Sickert appeared as a surprise witness in a BBC television series about the crimes. Sickert, who claimed to be the natural son of the painter Walter Sickert, told a most remarkable story. Apparently, Walter Sickert had been approached by Eddy's mother, Princess Alexandra of Denmark, with a view to guiding the Prince in to the world of art, where she felt his personality could grow, unstifled by his father and the Victorian court. Sickert's family moved closely within the royal circle and his father and grandfather had been artists to the Royal Court of Denmark. Sickert promised confidentiality. Neither the Queen nor Eddy's father would know of the arrangement.

At that time London's Tottenham Court Road had a Bohemian flavour, with its community of artists, writers and actors. The creative, the seekers-of-change, and the revolutionaries were there in abundance. It was to Sickert's rooms at 15, Cleveland Street, a large terraced house behind the great thoroughfare, that Eddy paid secret visits, passing himself off as the painter's younger brother Albert, and known to everyone as 'young Mr S.'.

Here, among artistic friends, the young prince blossomed. In the summer of 1884, the twenty-year-old Eddy was introduced by Sickert to a beautiful though illiterate young shopgirl who worked in the tobacconist's at number twenty-two. Eddy was immediately attracted to the lively, charming Midlands girl, whose name was Annie Elizabeth Crook.

In April the following year, Annie gave birth to a daughter by Eddy, Alice Margaret. Annie continued her work in the shop and lived a few doors away at number six. A girl she worked with was paid by Sickert to become the child's nanny. The royal affair was still secret, and it might have remained that way had not Eddy set even the friendliest tongues wagging by his next move.

At St Saviour's private chapel in neighbouring Osnaburgh Street, Eddy and Annie went through a Roman Catholic wedding ceremony. Whitehall was stunned by the rumours. Queen Victoria penned a furious note to her Prime Minister, the Marquess of Salisbury. The association must be stopped.

Salisbury saw the seeds of ferment and revolution increasing at an alarming speed, feeding on the poverty-stricken masses. There was a backlash against the Germanic Royal Family, and many thought Victoria would be the last monarch. There were those who despised what the sovereign stood for and there had even been assassination attempts. To the Irish she was known as 'the Famine Queen'. Her son's indiscretions and voracious sexual adventures only made the situation worse. The Conservatives had looked to the young Eddy for salvation, so popular was he with the common man, but these rumours could scotch all that. The tinder of anti-monarchic revolution was all around. Ireland, poverty and Socialism had seen to that. All the tinder needed to become a pyre was a spark. Eddy had seduced and married a Catholic and fathered a child by her, and Salisbury could almost smell the burning.

The Prime Minister knew that he must move quickly. The Prince and the girl must be parted. He entrusted the mission to Sir William Gull, Physician Extraordinary to Her Majesty. If Joseph Sickert is to be believed, Jack the Ripper was the seventy-two-year-old physician accompanied by the coachman and one other.

Annie and the Prince were kidnapped from the basement of 6, Cleveland Street. The Prince was returned to the royal court and Annie was taken to Guy's Hospital, where following an operation by Gull, she was rendered insane. A succession of mental institutions and work-houses followed, and she died in 1920.

If Lord Salisbury thought that with the kidnapping and brain operation the matter would be settled, he was in for a rude awakening. Joseph Sickert, recounting his father's tale, went on to tell of how the nanny who had looked after baby Alice had told the secret to a number of Whitechapel prostitutes. Between them they devised a blackmail plan.

The nanny was Mary Kelly. The accomplices in the ambitious blackmail plan were Nichols, Chapman and Stride. The physician, the

Annie Crook, the young tobacconist's assistant who found favour with a prince. She is said to have undergone surgery by Sir William Gull in an effort to erase her dangerous secrets. Buckingham Palace still denies the allegation that linked her with the Duke of Clarence.

coachman and another, leapt into action. And the rest is history.

Could, would, a government carry out such a Machiavellian plan? Author Stephen Knight, whose meetings with Sickert Jnr were recounted in his book *Jack the Ripper – The Final Solution* (Harrap, 1976) said, 'It all sounded terribly unlikely.' But two years of research subsequently convinced him of the truth of the story. Fact after fact was unearthed: Sickert's address; his connection with the Royal Family; birth certificates; certificates of insanity. And Sickert Snr, who had died in 1942, still would not lie down. There was more. He had told his son that the baby Alice, the daughter of the Prince and the shopgirl, had become his ward, and later, his mistress. She bore him a child, and it was to this son, Joseph, that the story was told.

Of John Netley, the coachman, little is known. It is said that he twice tried to run down young Alice with his coach. On 26 September 1903 the following report appeared in the *Marylebone Mercury and West London Gazette*:

> An inquest was held on the body of John Netley, forty-three. Evidence was given to the effect that the deceased was in the employ of Messrs Thompson and McKay, carmen to the Great Central Railway Company.
>
> On Sunday afternoon he was driving one of their pair of horse vans along Park Road, Regent's Park, when one of the wheels collided with a stone rest, and he was thrown from his seat into the roadway. As the deceased lay on the ground, one of the horses kicked him on the head and the wheel passed over him. He had no strap around him.
>
> Dr Norris, of 25, Park Road, said he was called and saw the deceased lying dead in the roadway near Clarence Gate. There were extensive injuries to the head. Death, which was due to fracture of the skull, was instantaneous. The jury returned a verdict of accidental death.

The jury seemed to have been in no doubt. Accidents happened then as now, so it is idle to speculate whether silence was again being enforced by violent means.

The old surgeon, Gull, dropped out of society about a year after the murders and died in January 1890, apparently of a stroke.

And what of the third man? Walter Sickert had made the startling claim that the final member of the trio had been none other than Sir Robert Anderson. Like Salisbury and Sir Charles Warren he was a leading Freemason, and he had been appointed head of CID on the eve of Polly Nichols' murder. However, Knight's researches showed that the third man was not the police chief. The third point in the triangle, his silence bought by a £500 bribe from Salisbury, was Sickert himself.

On 25 June 1976, under the headline 'A son's burden of truth', the *London Evening News* gave Joseph Sickert what they thought was the last word:

> At last the burden of knowledge I have carried for so long has been lifted from me. In a strange sort of way my mother and grand-mother have been revenged. Those who caused their suffering are now named. They cannot hide their guilty faces from the world any longer.
>
> Also the stain is cleansed from the families of men who have been named by various authors in the past as the Whitechapel killer. They owe their gratitude to Stephen Knight, who has brought the true story to light.
>
> When the author told me his conclusions about my father's involvement in the case I was angry. I felt he had let me down and betrayed my trust. But later I had to admit that my father must have known more than he told me. It was a fact that I had half realized all along.

That, you may think, would have given to succeeding generations of Ripperologists sufficient grist to their respective mills. However, the route to the Ripper is nothing if not tortuous. Two years later the following newspaper headline once more threw everything into question:

JACK THE RIPPER SOLUTION A HOAX – MAN
CONFESSES.
                                    (*Sunday Times*, 18 June 1978)

This was Joseph Sickert, now reported as saying; 'It was a hoax. I made it all up ... a whopping fib'. He stuck to the part about his parentage, but the Ripper story, he said, was pure invention. 'As an artist I found it easy to paint Jack the Ripper into the story.'

Stephen Knight was quick to answer. 'Sickert Snr *was* the third man, not Anderson, as he Sickert had claimed.' It had, said Knight, been this deviation from Walter Sickert's original story that had so incensed his son, who had felt betrayed. 'He begged me not to publish my findings, he would deny the whole story. But I had his signed statement.'

To return for a moment to the 'Masonic Connection' hypothesis, Sir William Gull's membership of the worldwide brotherhood of Freemasons prompted Stephen Knight to suggest another aspect to his theory. He postulated that following Lord Salisbury's fears of anarchic revolution, which would undoubtedly have removed not only the monarchy but Freemasonry as well, the active and dedicated Freemason Gull decided to carry out the murders as a Masonic ritual, possibly with the assistance of Netley the coachman and Sir Robert Anderson. (Or was it Sickert?)

If this version is accepted, that Gull was the Ripper alone, or that he headed a state-endorsed trio, it raises a number of questions. Why would Gull have made his dangerous task more hazardous by writing Masonic rituals into the scenario of the crimes? Was he prompted by the legend of the three apprentice Masons accused of murdering the Grand Master in charge of building Solomon's Temple? Their victim had been found with abdomen slashed open and entrails grouped, Ripper-style, on the shoulders of the corpse. It was said that the word 'Juwes' in the message which Warren had personally removed with such alacrity referred not to Jews, but to Juwes – the three legendary killers.

Illogical perhaps. But there are many other theories that can be sacrificed on the altar of logic. Whoever said mass-murder has to be logical? Was the terrible trio Gull, Netley and Anderson, or was Sickert the 'third man'? Could Gull have been a lone killer of those wretched women? Of all the Ripper threads, this is truly a tangled skein.

The lodgers

1 AN UNKNOWN VETERINARY STUDENT

Although the artist's story only became public in 1973, Walter Sickert's name had been mentioned many years before in connection, albeit innocent, with the Whitechapel killings. This version of the story has Sickert renting a room in the East End whose landlady told him of the previous occupant, a veterinary student who would often get home at dawn, to pace around endlessly until the morning papers were on sale.

The landlady and her husband would hear the student returning with the papers. Later, the old man would see traces of the student's clothing in the fireplace, where the lodger had burnt his suit of the night before. Before they could make up their minds to report their suspicions to the police, the student's mother came and collected him. He had always appeared sick and delicate, and she was taking him back to the family home in Bournemouth. From that moment the murders stopped.

Did this really happen to Sickert? an unsubstantiated tale, told by Sickert himself, could it have been a decoy to cover the tracks of Gull, Netley and (if he was the third man), Sickert himself?

11 G. WENTWORTH-BELL

G. Wentworth-Bell was a Canadian renting a bed-sitting room at 27, Sun Street, Finsbury Square. A solicitor by profession, he was a fundraiser for the Toronto Trust Society. He was seen by the landlady to keep three loaded revolvers in his bureau. He was something of a religious zealot and hated prostitutes, proclaiming loudly that they should be drowned, and he would read to his landlord from a hatred-filled notebook.

On the night that Martha Tabram was killed he was said to have crept home at 4 a.m. Next morning, bloodstained sheets together with the 'evidence' of several suits and pairs of rubber-soled shoes convinced the landlord that his lodger was the Ripper.

Although definitely resident in Finsbury Square in 1888, the lodger was gone later that year, saying that he was returning to Canada. He was never traced.

This social misfit was to become the prototype of the stealthy lodger in countless stories and films. Magazine articles in the early 1900s were followed by Hitchcock's silent film *The Lodger* in the late 1920s.

The shadow that hangs over this lodger theory is that its originator, Dr L. Forbes-Winslow, a self-styled medical theorist and practical detective, claimed that he told the police of his theory in 1889. He had offered a simple ambush plan which they had refused to take seriously. No police record exists.

GULL, Sir William (alternative theory)

Baronet and Physician Extraordinary to the Queen.
Physician in Ordinary to the Prince of Wales and the Royal Family

We have seen that one theory involves Sir William Gull as part of a trio of murderers; but there is another theory which gives the good Doctor the starring role.

At the time of the first Ripper murder a journalist named Robert Lees was working in Fleet Street. From the first murder to the last, and right up to the time of his death in January 1931, he claimed to know the identity of Jack the Ripper. One journalist's claims are no better than another's, but Lees was not only a journalist, he was also a distinguished Spiritualist, considered to be one of the leading mediums of his day.

After her husband's death in 1868 Queen Victoria had consulted

Lees, and he had held seances in an attempt to contact the Prince Consort. The Queen was also known to be intensely interested in identifying the Whitechapel murderer, though her reasons were not stated.

Lees predicted the first three murders and described them in detail. His foreknowledge of the dates on which the Ripper would claim another victim so frightened him that he fled to Europe. He frequently contacted Scotland Yard but the police would not listen.

After one vision, in which Lees had seen a victim with mutilated ears, the police listened more attentively to his claims. His vision coincided with a letter received by the police in which identical mutilation threats had been made. His premonition of Mary Kelly's death was taken very seriously by the police.

After the murder of Mary Kelly, Lees was taken to Miller's Court and was used as a human bloodhound, taking detectives to an elegant West End house, the home of a leading physician.

Here the story takes a less definite turn. In one version, the detectives questioned the physician's wife, finding out that he had been torturing the cat, beating his small son, and staying out on the nights of murders. Clothes in the physician's wardrobe were identical to those seen in Lees's visions.

A specially formed commission certified the man insane. To account for his disappearance, his sudden death was announced, and a bogus funeral with a stone-weighted coffin was staged. The surgeon is said to have died many years later in an asylum.

In another version, Dr Thomas Stowell, examining Gull's personal papers, speculated whether the house which Lees found was 74, Brook Street, Mayfair, home of Sir William Gull. Gull's daughter had spoken of her mother's questioning by police. Was this, Stowell wondered, a valiant attempt to divert suspicion from Eddy?

What is certain is that Sir William had a slight stroke the year before the Ripper murders and gave up medical practice. He was seventy years old and had no young son. (His son was grown up.) Gull's death certificate, dated 1890, gives the cause of death as a stroke.

STEPHEN, James Kenneth

Tutor to the Duke of Clarence
b ?
d 3 February 1892

James Kenneth Stephen, youthful tutor to the Duke of Clarence while at Cambridge, came under suspicion by writer Michael Harrison in his biography of the Duke.

Harrison recalled that Dr Stowell, in his examination of Sir William Gull's papers had come across many references to a leading figure – believed to be the Ripper and referred to as 'S'. To the day he died, Stowell, pestered by journalists and grilled on television, never confirmed publicly that 'S' *was* the Duke of Clarence. However, he was not against dropping outrageous hints which pointed unmistakably in the direction of the Palace.

Harrison, researching the Duke's biography, did not believe this. He produced the interesting theory that Stowell, in referring to 'S', was actually quoting verbatim from Gull's records. In other words, Gull himself had only referred to his suspect as 'S' and Stowell had drawn the wrong conclusion.

The initial 'S', conjectured Harrison, need not have been Clarence at all, but could well have referred to a close friend. His efforts to find someone who had been a close friend of the Duke and whose career fitted the facts was soon rewarded. The trail led unmistakably to James Stephen.

Stephen was known to be an obsessive misogynist. Many of Stephen's poems are quoted in full in *Clarence* and his quirk is given rein in many of them. The poems reveal not only his vitriolic hatred of women but also his growing psychosis, said to have been worsened by a violent blow on the head, which delivered him to an asylum where he died in 1892.

One verse, packed with insane hatred, ended with these lines:

> May fiends with glowing pincers rend thy brain,
> And beetles batten on thy blackened face

This reflection of sadistic violence was prompted by a train passenger's accidental treading on Stephen's foot.

Whether Stephen was Clarence's lover is not certain, but if this was so, the affair had certainly cooled by the time the Duke left Cambridge to join the 10th Hussars. Two years later, a serious head injury left Stephen with brain damage. He seemed to recover, but the injury was permanent. It was as a result of this accident that Stephen became a patient of Dr Gull.

His suspected relationship with the Duke finished, Stephen is thought by Harrison to have turned instead to murdering in Whitechapel. But if this was revenge for being jilted by his homosexual lover, why women, and why Whitechapel?

Harrison's theory is based on ten murders, all committed on royal anniversaries and seen by Harrison possibly as blood sacrifices, offered up by the perverted genius of a psychopath.

Stephen was certified insane in 1891 and died in an asylum.

Was James Kenneth Stephen the Ripper? We may never know. Stowell's conjectures on the initial 'S' could be tested by reference to Gull's papers, but unfortunately they were destroyed by his family in the 1930s.

Jill the Ripper

The prospect of the Ripper being female was considered by the *Illustrated Police News*, not noted for its conservatism, and rejected:

> As the plot of the Whitechapel murders thickens, in the sense of them being more and more difficult to solve, the suggestions grow wilder and wilder. Dr Forbes Winslow's idea that the man is a gentleman living in the West End and only going out to vivisect people at intervals, after which he forgets all about it, was startling enough. Now we are asked whether we should be surprised to hear that the malefactor is a female. He thinks this quite within the range of probability.
>
> If we associate this ingenious supposition with that of Dr Winslow we get a lady fiend, living in the West End, and indulging in those homicidal acts perhaps after a drawing-room reading from Browning. One may, of course, suppose anything; but we really do think these flights of fancy rise to an atmosphere in which commonsense finds some difficulty in breathing.

The biggest question mark hanging over the suggestion that the Whitechapel fiend was not male but female, is the one posed by many investigators – could a woman possibly have carried out such heinous deeds? There are in fact several cases of women having committed equally terrible murders.

Early this century a Frenchwoman named Jeanne Webber was convicted of brutally killing at least five children including her own son. She died in the lunatic asylum at Mareville.

In June 1860 Constance Kent was only sixteen years old when she decapitated her half-brother, four-year-old Francis Saville Kent. No motive has ever been established. The death sentence was commuted and she was released from prison in 1885. (It is odd how royal links recur in our trail. Constance's father, Samuel Saville Kent, deputy inspector of factories, was reputed to be the illegitimate son of the Duke of Kent, father of Queen Victoria.)

The turnover at Nurse Culligan's old people's home in Hartford, Connecticut, USA, was remarkable. Inmates departed this life at more than 6½ times the Hartford average rate for 1914. Nurse Culligan may have poisoned as many as twenty. Four, including her husband, were exhumed, and all had died from arsenic. Life imprisonment followed for Nurse Culligan and in 1923 she was declared insane.

LaFarge, Bartlett, Crawford, Smith, Hindley – all loom large in a catalogue of cold-blooded murderesses. Not all of them were frenzied mass-killers admittedly, but every one was representative of the gentler sex at its least gentle.

The theory that Jack was in fact Jill has had many advocates. No less a literary sleuth than Sir Arthur Conan Doyle MD believed that the killings were the revenge of a berserk midwife-abortionist who had been turned in by a prostitute. On release from prison the midwife's revenge was accomplished by tearing out the organs of her erstwhile clients.

In a *Sun* newspaper reappraisal of the crimes in 1972, Arthur Butler offered a novel variation on the theme. Butler argued that there had been seven killings, committed by not one but *two* Rippers, Jack and Jill. Described as an ex-Scotland Yard Chief and as one of the top detectives of our time, the *Sun* credited Butler with eight solved murders. (Less successful investigations were not enumerated.)

According to Butler, Jill was an abortionist, by appointment to the street-women of Whitechapel. When four prostitutes died as a result of her botched surgery, she mutilated them to hide the evidence. Her accomplice murdered the other women to silence them.

The Yard man's story is enlivened by details of the small-part characters in the drama, though credibility is stretched by the introduction of characters with names like Fingers Freddy. Jack and Jill went out to kill?

In July 1971 the magazine *Weekend* contained the following extraordinary headline:

MY WIFE WAS JACK THE RIPPER

This remarkable claim headed a piece by reporter Richard Herd, who claimed to have been summoned to the home of a dying octogenarian some years before.

The man Herd interviewed was a sailor who had married a lovely nurse from the London Hospital in Whitechapel on the day before his final voyage. When he returned he intended to seek work as a porter at the hospital. At the end of the voyage he and his shipmates were drinking at a dockside pub. Two prostitutes joined them and he and his friend left with them.

His wife saw him return with the prostitute and, supposedly, some time later began the series of crimes, using a carving knife from the wedding set given her by friends at the hospital. When the sailor was confronted by bloody knives and bloodstained seaman's trousers in the sink, his wife confessed to him. She told him of her disguise as a sailor, her carpet-bag concealing her murse's clothes, and the carver. Apparently her victims would greet her as a sailor. She then murdered and mutilated them, making off with her hospital cloak and bonnet over the sailor suit.

Credible, or an old lag's tale, concocted to while away the years at Parkhurst? The informant was a convicted forger, whose talents with the large old copperplate-style £5 notes had resulted in a score of wasted years in which to think.

Taken literally, the *Weekend* story of 1971 has a most peculiar ring, for it has Herd being told the tale of an eighty-four year old dying penman in November 1965. These ages and dates would have made our sailor just seven years old at the time of the murders – precocious indeed, even for Whitechapel!

Assuming 1965 is a misprint for 1945, then we have a twenty-seven year old sailor and the story is rather more plausible. Or is it?

Butcher/Slaughterman

That Jack – or Jill – was a butcher there is no doubt, but was he or she actually *a butcher by trade*? By the time of the Whitechapel murders, Tsarist pogroms had caused many Eastern European Jews to flee and settle in the East End. There was considerable concern amongst the Jewish community that the street panic engendered by the killings would result in similar persecution in England.

Matters were not helped when the following appeared in *The Times* on 2 October:

THE WHITECHAPEL MURDERS

Vienna. 1 Oct.
With reference to the recent atrocious murders in London, attention may be called to a similar crime which preoccupied the public in this country for nearly three years. A Galician Jew named Ritter

was accused in 1884 of having murdered and mutilated a Christian woman in a village near Cracow.

The mutilation was like that perpetrated on the body of the woman Chapman, and at the trial numbers of witnesses deposed that among certain fanatical Jews there existed a superstition to the effect that if a Jew became intimate with a Christian woman he would atone for his offence by slaying and mutilating the object of his passion.

Sundry passages of the Talmud were quoted which, according to the witnesses, expressly sanctioned this form of atonement. The trial caused an immense sensation, and Ritter was sentenced to death.

The correspondent went on to tell how the Court of Appeal, feeling that the man was a victim of anti-Semitic prejudice, ordered a re-trial. Again the jury pronounced against Ritter. Once again the Court of Appeal found a flaw and a third trial, with a verdict of guilty, condemned the man to death. The Court of Appeal then quashed the sentence, and Ritter was released having been in prison for three years.

The office of the Chief Rabbi was appalled by the newspaper report. There was no such superstition that in certain circumstances a Jew might be justified in slaying a Christian woman. Ritter had been accused in an atmosphere of anti-Semitism and had ultimately been acquitted.

> The tragedies enacted in the East End are sufficiently distressing, without the revival of moribund fables and the importation of prejudices abhorrent to the English nation.

The Chief Rabbi's concern was understandable, but Jews became increasingly suspected in the emotion-charged atmosphere of the streets. Rumour told of harsh Talmudic law where harlotry was concerned – how whores had been punished by stoning or strangulation. Additionally, the inhabitants of Whitechapel were quick to note similarities in Jewish slaughter methods to the way in which the victims had been butchered. Old Testament ritual includes cutting the animal's throat and conducting a post-mortem by incision in the chest and abdomen, the latter to facilitate examination of the intestines, kidneys and internal organs. Meat was judged either imperfect and forbidden, or certified edible and 'kosher'.

Whitechapel was home to a large Jewish community, and there were many *shochets*, ritual slaughtermen who were also minor religious figures. All would have possessed the skill and instruments to perform the Ripper's fiendish work.

Some newspaper correspondents observed that the traditional dark dress of the Jewish cleric matched that mentioned in some of the descriptions of suspects.

But it was not just the Jewish religious slaughtermen who possessed the necessary skills to murder like Jack. The Home Office files contain a letter from a retired butcher who claimed that he could kill and dress five sheep in an hour. He had never seen the inside of a human, but presumed it to be similar to a sheep or pig. He pointed out that a skilful butcher would get little blood on his clothes. 'There has been nothing done yet to any of these poor women that an expert butcher could not do almost in the dark.'

A religious *shochet* or master butcher might have the necessary skills, but why should he want to commit such terrible crimes? This is a candidature which is strong on method but light on motive.

An alternative ritual theory is that concerning the Russian religious sect that practised self-mutilation in the belief that asexuals would eventually rule the world. The Skoptsi sect was active in Russia for about 150 years, up to the turn of the twentieth century, when its influence had spread beyond its borders into Finland.

The chief feature of the Skoptsi's initiation rituals was known as 'greater and lesser baptisms of fire'. These baptisms comprised castration, hysterectomy and mastectomy, and perhaps understandably had few takers, being undergone by only a small minority of novitiates. The self-mutilating sect is known to have practised widely in Russia, as recently as the early 1930s. Former Soviet Premier, George Malenkov, was allegedly a Skoptsi, and his masculinity, or lack of it, has been commented on by several writers.

Whitechapel had a large Russian population, and there is a theory that a Skoptsi member was the Ripper, believing he was saving the souls of whores by obligingly offering them the 'greater baptism of fire'.

Jack the Ripper – ritual slaughterer, master butcher or religious zealot? These are not modern theories. In the East End in the autumn of 1888 such rumours were rife, prompting one anonymous poet to achieve posterity in the famous – and sadly unattributed:

> I'm not a butcher
> Nor a Yid,
> Nor yet a foreigner skipper,
> But I'm your own lighthearted friend,
> Yours truly Jack the Ripper

Bill the Ripper

The 'Old Bill', cockney parlance for the police, has not escaped the attention of Ripper-seekers. Many investigators have argued that the close cordons put around Whitechapel, and the obvious attention that would have been paid to any stranger in the relatively close-knit community at that time of fear and suspicion, narrow the search to a particular group. Only someone with a good reason to be found near a body, capable of moving around freely at night, possibly in blood-stained clothing, with elementary surgery knowledge, could fit this group.

Nurses, midwifes, and slaughtermen, are all obvious candidates. So too are policemen, and they were thick on the ground. Uniformed police, plain-clothes detectives, police in women's clothing. All had the opportunity.

Contemporary records show a number of attacks on police, though doubtless not all were prompted by suspicions that they were the Ripper. One report tells of the unpleasant experience of the police detective-sergeant who on 25 October in Phoenix Place, St Pancras was punched in the eye by a cab driver. The sergeant was dressed entirely as a woman. We are not told whether he was on duty at the time.

Donald Rumbelow, himself a City policeman, reminds us in *The Complete Jack the Ripper* that policemen were recruited mainly from ex-soldiers whose years of war overseas would certainly have given them an experience of slaughter, of both men and horses, and a rudimentary knowledge of first aid.

Although hundreds of extra police were present in Whitechapel, that they were not always perceived to be so may be accounted for by the numerous reports of H Division officers being disguised as nurses and slaughtermen. However, the police charades perplexed Jack not a bit. It was at the height of their attempts at disguises that he committed two murders within minutes of each other, both in the very streets in which, if the accounts are to be believed, slaughtermen with truncheons and nurses in size ten boots were practically falling over each other ...

The Doctors

Dr Stanley	Dr Mikhail Ostrog
Dr Merchant	Dr Vassily Konavalov
Dr Alexander Pedachenko	Dr Thomas Neill Cream

DR STANLEY

In the first full-length book on the murders, *The Mystery of Jack the Ripper* (W. H. Allen, 1929) MP Leonard Matters suggested the theory of a Harley Street surgeon whose son had died of the then incurable syphilis, which he had supposedly caught from Mary Kelly. The surgeon's revenge trail encompassed four other prostitutes before he settled his terrible account in Miller's Court.

Although Matters claimed that this was the content of the doctor's death-bed confession in Buenos Aires, no Dr Stanley has ever been traced. It is unlikely that Dr Stanley would have taken some months to find Mary Kelly, who was so well known in the area.

DR MERCHANT

PC Robert Spicer was puzzled. He had noticed the smartly-dressed man with rosy cheeks earlier that evening. Who was the well-dressed professional type, complete with Gladstone bag, seated on the dustbin with a local prostitute?

Although the woman made no complaint against him the constable took the stranger to the police station. There the inspectors were inclined to the view that he was a philanthropist helping fallen women. The man proved his identity as a doctor from Brixton in south London, and was released.

Many years later, when he had left the force, Robert Spicer published an account of his 'Ripper' in the *Daily Express*. In 1972, enthusiastic Ripperologist Brian Reilly described how this snippet of information in a 1931 newspaper had set him on the trail of the Brixton doctor.

Beginning with the description of the anonymous, smartly-dressed doctor, Reilly had fleshed out the shadowy details of PC Spicer's suspect into 'Dr Merchant', who had died of tuberculosis in a London hospital in December 1888, a few weeks after the Mary Kelly killing.

Reilly describes the symptoms of tuberculosis as including rosy cheeks and pictures the mortally ill doctor running amok amongst the social outcasts of Whitechapel. Reilly's suspect was thirty-seven years old and had a history of mental instability, perhaps caused by childhood memories of the Indian Mutiny when his father, a non-commissioned officer in the British Army, dispatched mutineers by firing them from the barrels of cannon. Could these gruesome executions have had a lasting impression on the boy, so that in later years, ravaged by mortal illness, he found victims to execute and at the same time an outlet for his under-used surgical skills? Reilly's research was painstaking and he claims his theory is at least as good as any other.

DR PEDACHENKO (also known as Mikhail Ostrog and Vassily Konavalov)

A theory that includes double-dealing by the Russian police and a mad doctor with three aliases was strongly advanced by Donald McCormick in his *The Identity of Jack the Ripper*, published in 1970. It is a more than usually complicated strand in the tortuous tales that surround the shadowy killer, and it has a number of variations.

The theory is based on a manuscript said to have been written in French by Rasputin, the Russian monk who was assassinated in 1917, and found in his effects after his death. A lunatic doctor, having murdered several women in his birthplace, the Russian town of Tver, is sent by the Ochrana, the Russian secret police, to London. Here he sets about killing prostitutes so that he can record the ineptitude of Scotland Yard, and embarrass the British government. The doctor's work in Tver Maternity Hospital, together with his known homicidal tendencies, were excellent credentials for this diplomatic mission.

According to the Rasputin manuscript, a man called Nideroest, well known in London as a Russian secret police spy and member of the Anarchists' Centre in east London, disclosed the true author of the crimes. The identity of the Whitechapel killer had been revealed to him in the anarchists' club one night by an old Russian subversive, Nicholas Zverieff. He named Pedachenko. The report in London soon reached the ears of the Russians and was thus reported in a confidential secret police fortnightly gazette in January 1909:

> The report of Nideroest's discovery amused our Secret Police greatly, for, as a matter of fact, they knew the whole details at the time, and had themselves actively encouraged and aided the crimes, in order to exhibit to the world certain defects of the English police system.
>
> It was indeed for that reason that Pedachenko, the greatest and boldest of all Russian lunatics, was encouraged to go to London and commit that series of atrocious crimes, in which agents of our police aided him.
>
> Such are the actual facts of the Jack the Ripper mystery which still puzzles the world.

For those theorists who look to the abrupt termination of the murders as symptomatic of the death of the culprit, or incarceration in a mental home, Pedachenko serves well. He disappeared after the Kelly murder and was caught while mutilating a woman he had killed in St Petersburg in 1891. He died in an asylum in 1908.

Pedachenko, Ostrog and Konavalov were all medical practitioners and are generally assumed to have been the same person. Ostrog was one of three suspects mentioned in the Macnaghten notes written in 1903:

> Michael Ostrog, a Russian doctor, and a convict, who was subsequently detained in a lunatic asylum as a homicidal maniac. This man's antecedents were of the worst possible type, and his whereabouts at the time of the murders could never be ascertained.

McCormick's fascinating account of this theory includes the following description of Pedachenko/Ostrog:

> Born: 1857
> Height: medium
> Eyes: dark blue
> Profession: junior surgeon
> General description: Usually wore black moustache curled and waxed at ends. Heavy black eyebrows. Broad shouldered but slight build. Known to disguise himself as woman on occasions and in women's clothes when arrested in Petrograd before his detention in the asylum where he died.

McCormick writes convincingly of his conviction that this is Jack. Leaving aside any temptation to fantasize some kind of Groucho Marx, stalking the streets of Whitechapel in drag, it has to be admitted that this description – *sans* feminine attire – matches the principal sightings very closely.

DR THOMAS NEILL CREAM
b Glasgow 27 May 1850
d 15 November 1892

Strychnine had killed Ellen Donworth. Though only nineteen, she was a well-known prostitute in Duke Street, Westminster Bridge Road, where she had lived. A week later, in the autumn of 1891, a twenty-six-year-old prostitute, Matilda Clover, was poisoned. Some months later, two more young street-walkers died in agony, both on the same day. Emma Shrivell and Alice Marsh both lived in second-floor rooms at 118, Stamford Street, a brothel at the Elephant and Castle. They had been poisoned, and as a result of what they told police before they died, newspapers began to speculate on the identity of the Lambeth poisoner. Could he be Jack the Ripper?

In the spring of 1892, more than two years after the slaying of Mary Kelly, London still twitched uncomfortably at Jack's memory. There had been other killings attributed to the Ripper, including that of

Frances Coles, found under a railway arch a year before with her throat slit and her flesh slashed and mutilated in the all too familiar manner. A man had been arrested almost immediately, but after several remands had been released. Could the monstrous butcher now have changed his methods?

Responsibility for the poisonings would eventually be laid at the door of Dr Thomas Neill Cream. Born in Glasgow in 1850, Cream's family had emigrated to Canada when he was thirteen. There he had graduated in medicine at McGill University in 1876, but had quickly found a life of fraud, blackmail and attempted murder more appealing. At least four women, including his wife, died under his care.

In 1881, the law finally caught up with him and he was sentenced to life imprisonment at Joliet Prison, Illinois. He was released in 1891 and arrived in England on 1 October. Ellen Donworth died on the thirteenth, and Matilda, a week later.

Cream was something of a wordsmith who enjoyed taunting the police about his crimes, as so many murderers had done before and have done since. The pitiless sadist revelled in drawing attention to his exploits. Letters giving clues were received by the Coroner and others. Some years ago a leading graphologist, Donald Davis, asserted that he had no doubt whatsoever that two of the 'Ripper letters' had been written by Cream.

One of the poisoner's letters led the police to a potential victim who had not swallowed the proffered pills but had secreted them in her hand and thrown them in the Thames when her client was not looking. She described the man as about 5 ft 9 in in height, balding, broad shouldered, and of stout build. One of the most noteworthy things about him was his cross-eyes, which peered out from behind thick glasses. He was expensively dressed and wore a tall hat.

The police investigation that followed was painstaking and on 3 June 1892, three weeks after the murders of Emma and Alice, Cream was arrested. In October he was tried at the Old Bailey and went to the scaffold at Newgate Prison on 15 November, where he gave his final message to a startled hangman Billington. As the bolt was drawn, his words 'I am Jack the . . .' wrote another question mark in the Ripper file.

There is no reason to suppose that the executioner would have invented this tale. Twenty years earlier the announcement would have been to the public at large, for until 1868 executions were carried out publicly, outside the prison walls.

The astute reader will have noticed that at the time of the five

Whitechapel crimes Dr Cream was apparently serving ten years of a life sentence in Illinois. Oh foolish reader! By now you should know the trail of the Ripper is littered with such red herrings.

Many years before, Cream had been defended on a bigamy charge by Sir Edward Marshall Hall, who advised him to plead guilty. Cream refused. His alibi was one of mistaken identity. He had, he claimed, been in prison in Australia at the time of the alleged offence. The prison confirmed that a man answering Cream's description had been an inmate at that time.

Edward Marjoribanks, Marshall Hall's biographer (*The Life of Sir Edward Marshall Hall*; Gollancz 1929) recorded that the great advocate had a theory that Neill Cream used the same name as a double in the underworld, and each used the terms of imprisonment of the other as an alibi, whenever there was a need.

So, theoretically, at the time that 'Doctor Cream' was committing the murders in the East End, the other Cream was inmate number 4274 in Joliet State Prison. 'Doctor Cream' had got off the bigamy charge thanks to his double's circumstances at the time, and how those last words on the scaffold would repay the debt.

So it would seem pretty conclusive that Cream did not commit the Whitechapel crimes, but the possibility of a double, another 'Dr Cream', is not ruled out by many who see in this evil, but extraordinary poisoner, a link to the murders and mutilations in the East End.

DEEMING, *Frederick Bailey*

b *c.* 1842
d 23 May 1892
General description: Large, muscular, hard-faced, handsome, man. Fair hair and moustache. Light-blue eyes. Posed as aristocrat.

In the Black Museum at Scotland Yard there is a plaster death-mask of Frederick Deeming which was for many years pointed out as the face of Jack the Ripper. Deeming was under sentence of death in the spring of 1892 when he confessed to being Jack the Ripper. He argued in court that murder in certain circumstances was perfectly permissible. He had himself gone out with a revolver to kill a woman who had infected him with VD. He considered that such women should be exterminated.

Deeming had been tried for the murder of his second wife just before Christmas 1891. Her body had been found cemented under the dining-room floor in their home in Melbourne, Australia – her throat had been cut. On the other side of the world, a few months later, the remains of his first wife and four children were found cemented beneath the floors of a previous residence in Rainhill, near Liverpool. The venereal disease may have unhinged his mind, but when found guilty he was sane enough to telegraph a notice of appeal to the Privy Council in London.

Marshall Hall assisted the great barrister Geogeghan in representing the petition to the noble and learned Lords under the presidency of Lord Halisbury.

Geogeghan was a powerful, natural orator who disliked interruption. As the great Privy Council chamber was echoing with the unaccustomed sound of his Irish brogue, an important telegram arrived. Several times Marshall Hall tried to attract his senior's attention. The Irish patience soon snapped. 'Don't dare to interrupt me when I'm addressing this court', he whispered furiously. Geogeghan continued his speech and eventually the court adjourned for lunch. 'Why did you interrupt me like that?' asked the Irishman. Silently Marshall Hall handed him the telegram, it was from the prison chaplain in Australia, and it read: 'Deeming hanged this morning'.

Years later, Marshall Hall said that he had no doubt that this experience of pleading for the life of a man already dead was a unique experience, and Geogeghan never visited the Privy Council again.

The memoirs that Deeming penned in the death cell denied the crime of which he stood convicted but declared that he was Jack the Ripper. The notes, and all his papers, were destroyed after his death.

Gordon Honeycombe, author of *Murders of the Black Museum* (Hutchinson, 1982), reports an air of mardi-gras in the Melbourne prison on the morning of Monday, 23 May 1892. A large crowd of ticket-holding officials saw Deeming walk to the scaffold. He was smoking a large cigar and was accompanied by executioners who, in a commendable effort at self-effacement, were wearing false beards.

The chaplain gave the hooded prisoner an unexpected four minutes' grace by reading the entire burial service before the bolts were drawn.

To the last, Deeming never retracted his 'confession'.

PIZER, Jack (John)

b 1855
General description: 5 ft tall, dark swarthy face, unpleasant to look at because of grizzly black strips of hair, nearly an inch in length, which

cover his face. Cruel, sardonic look. Drooping moustache and side-whiskers. Large head, heavy neck. A person of repellent appearance which is not in any way refined by his splay-footed gait and thick foreign accent. Is known as 'Leather Apron', often called at Commercial Road lodgings and asked for certain girls by name.

(*East London Observer*)

POLICE NOTICE

John Pizer, otherwise known as 'Leather Apron', is a man of Jewish forebears, and lives at 22, Mulberry Street, with his stepmother aged seventy, and his married brother, whose name is Gabriel. Pizer is thirty-four and by trade is a mender of leather shoes and book bindings. The police, in questioning Mr Pizer about the murder of Annie Chapman, have confiscated five sharp knives and a collection of hats. He is a man of slight build but strong shoulders, 5 ft 5 in tall, with a dark beard and side-whiskers. His chin is clean-shaven. He walks with a slight stoop and talks in a low intimate voice.

The police are interested in confirming his whereabouts on the night of 30 August and on the night of 7 September. Anyone who might have information concerning this man should report to the Leman Street police station at once.

J. H. Sides,
Sergeant, H Division
Metropolitan Police

When this police notice was circulated in September 1888, with clear reference to the Nichols and Chapman killings, it was greeted with some relief by the inhabitants of Whitechapel.

Following the first murder, police enquiries revealed that a man named Jack Pizer had been ill-treating prostitutes in the area. Initial suspicion hardened when, after the second murder, a piece of leather apron was found close to the scene. Pizer was known as 'Leather Apron'.

The arrest of the Polish Jew on 10 September was short-lived. Pizer's alibi was that he had remained indoors at 22, Mulberry Street for an entire week beginning two days before Chapman's murder. He did so, he claimed, because of the strong anti-Semitic feeling which arose following the killing of Polly Nichols. Police were quick to note that whilst his apprehension was understandable, as was his desire to keep a low profile, he could not possibly have had knowledge on the 6th that another murder was about to happen on the 8th.

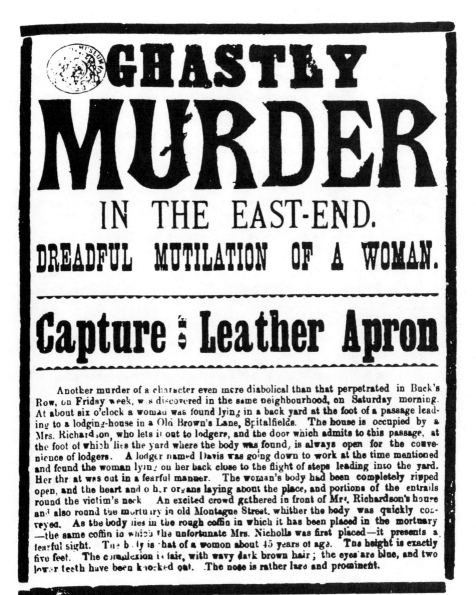

GHASTLY MURDER

IN THE EAST-END.

DREADFUL MUTILATION OF A WOMAN.

Capture of Leather Apron

Another murder of a character even more diabolical than that perpetrated in Buck's Row, on Friday week, was discovered in the same neighbourhood, on Saturday morning. At about six o'clock a woman was found lying in a back yard at the foot of a passage leading to a lodging-house in a Old Brown's Lane, Spitalfields. The house is occupied by a Mrs. Richardson, who lets it out to lodgers, and the door which admits to this passage, at the foot of which lies the yard where the body was found, is always open for the convenience of lodgers. A lodger named Davis was going down to work at the time mentioned and found the woman lying on her back close to the flight of steps leading into the yard. Her throat was cut in a fearful manner. The woman's body had been completely ripped open, and the heart and other organs laying about the place, and portions of the entrails round the victim's neck. An excited crowd gathered in front of Mrs. Richardson's house and also round the mortuary in old Montague Street, whither the body was quickly conveyed. As the body lies in the rough coffin in which it has been placed in the mortuary —the same coffin in which the unfortunate Mrs. Nicholls was first placed—it presents a tearful sight. The body is that of a woman about 45 years of age. The height is exactly five feet. The complexion is fair, with wavy dark brown hair; the eyes are blue, and two lower teeth have been knocked out. The nose is rather large and prominent.

The Times quoted Sergeant Sides:

> There is no doubt that he is the murderer, for a number of long-bladed knives and several hats were found in his possession.

Following his arrest by Detective Sergeant Thicke, five knives and a number of hats (which Pizer made) had been discovered. The millinery was significant, said police, because of Polly Nichols' proud remarks about her new hat. The police were confident. Flaws had been discovered in the cobbler's alibi. A witness, Emmanuel Violenia, half-Spanish, half-Bulgarian, was staying at a lodging-house in Hanbury Street. In the early hours of Saturday morning he had seen a man and woman quarrelling, and apparently the man had said he would kill the woman. However, Violenia could not identify the body of Chapman as the woman, although he was sure that Pizer was the man. There were contradictions in the story, and the police did not proceed on this evidence.

Pizer denied that he had been in Hanbury Street. He had, he said, walked alone for some five miles from Whitechapel to Seven Sisters Road, then returned along Holloway Road. By this time it was 2.15 a.m. Fourpence bought him a bed in lodgings at the Round House in Holloway Road, which seems strange considering he already had lodgings at Mulberry Street. The manager remembered admitting Pizer at about 2.15 a.m., three hours before Chapman was killed. Pizer slept until 11.00 a.m.

If true, this curious tale places Pizer away from the murder scene more surely than did his original alibi, which was supported by his mother and brother.

Pizer was a thoroughly frightened man. Newspapers were referring to him as 'half man, half beast . . . a ghoulish creature, stalking with deadly Jewish cunning.' Public feeling was running high. There was talk that the authorities were afraid that the crowds would lynch him. The police held him for a few more days, perhaps only for his own safety.

Pizer was called to give evidence at the inquest and, encouraged by the Coroner, allowed to tell the story of his alibi. Subsequently he began a series of libel actions against the newspapers and broadsheets which had reported his arrest and so harshly presumed his guilt.

Years later, in his memoirs (*The Lighter Side of my Official Life*, Hodder and Stoughton, 1910), Sir Robert Anderson declared that the identity of the Ripper was known in official circles. He would not name the man but intriguingly hinted at the suspect:

> I will merely add that the only person who ever had a good view of the murderer unhesitatingly identified the suspect the instant he was confronted with him, but he refused to give evidence against him. In saying that he was a Polish Jew I am merely stating a definitely established fact.

But as we have already seen, there was more than one Polish Jew under suspicion to whom this statement could have referred. What of Severin Antoniovich Klosowski, alias George Chapman?

MILES, Frank

b 1855
d ?

Oscar Wilde's friends were, in their time, accused of many things. One of them, Frank Miles, was thought to be the Ripper.

Miles, a homosexual artist, had met Wilde at Oxford and had subsequently lived with him for a short time in London, where Wilde had taken rooms at Salisbury Street, off the Strand.

In the early 1970s, Scottish researcher Thomas Toughill observed some interesting and hitherto unknown signs that Wilde may have known that Miles was the Ripper. Hints of this, said Toughill, were clear in Wilde's novel, *The Picture of Dorian Gray* (1891). A possible link between Miles and the Duke of Clarence was also claimed. (Miles' cousin was the Duke's equerry.)

Miles was a gifted artist, headed for greatness, and his exhibitions were attended by the famous. Unfortunately he also had a predilection for exhibiting himself to small girls. This got him into considerable difficulties, in which the influential Wilde was often called on to assist.

Miles' death in Bristol asylum was announced in the March 1888 issue of the *Magazine of Art*. However, Toughill's researches show that the 'general paralysis of the insane' that killed Miles did not in fact do so until June 1891.

Wilde, a Freemason despite his Catholicism, does not appear to have left any posthumous comment, and it is interesting to surmise that some of his other writings might give more definitive clues.

There have been other suspects, but these make up our list. Make your decision, but as you do so consider: who had the motive; who had the opportunity; and who could offer a reasonable excuse for being found late at night near a dead body?

In the final chapter, which follows, let us review all our candidates once more, and consider finally who was most likely to have been the culprit the police never caught.

14
Pick your Ripper

DRUITT, Montague Thomas

When Sir Melville Macnaghten mentioned three likely suspects in his famous notes, he first listed Druitt.

> ... Mr M. J. Druitt, said to be a doctor and of good family, who disappeared at the time of the Miller's Court murder, and whose body (which was said to have been upwards of a month in the water) was found in the Thames on 31 December – or about seven weeks after that murder. He was sexually insane and from private information I have little doubt but that his own family believed him to have been the murderer.

The dates of Druitt's cricket fixtures which show him taking wickets just hours after the murders are not alibis. Could he have slaughtered, then simply donned cricketer's whites and coolly played – and played superbly as the score-cards show? The answer has to be 'Yes' – there are equally strange circumstances behind murders on record.

When the police swore Albert Backert, of the Whitechapel Vigilance Committee, to secrecy and told him that the Ripper had been fished out of the river, they were clearly referring to Druitt. The description of the man seen by the young PC White is said to have been widely published, but the man was never found. Compare his description with the photograph of Druitt.

Some believe that the Druitt connection started with a conversation between Walter Sickert and Sir Melville Macnaghten in the Garrick Club. Sickert told the Yard chief about the lodger veterinarian, concluding with the fact that the man had been taken back to Bournemouth by his mother. Druitt, like the vet, had a widowed mother living in Bournemouth. The Macnaghten Papers were written several years after the crimes, and Macnaghten may well have taken these 'clues', arriving from different directions, and added them together to form his theory.

Unfortunately, whatever the reasons for his preference, Macnaghten is himself less certain about Druitt;

A much more rational and workable theory is that the murderer's brain gave way completely after Miller's Court and that he committed suicide or, less likely, was found to be so hopelessly insane by his relatives that, suspecting the worst, they confined him in a lunatic asylum.

There is no doubt that Druitt was found drowned, presumed to have committed suicide. Does this cryptic note suggest that even the Scotland Yard chief was doubtful about Druitt? If you selected Druitt as the Ripper you are in good company. Over the years he has been a firm favourite. Researchers of the calibre of Dan Farson, whose carefully-documented television programmes were seen in the early 1960s, were convinced that the culprit was the young barrister.

Score 75%

CHAPMAN, George
(Severin Antoniovich Klosowski)

Could a butcher become a poisoner? Inspector Abberline was in no doubt. He is said to have greeted Chapman's arrest by Inspector Godley with the words 'You've got Jack the Ripper at last!'

In his book *The Trial of George Chapman* (Wm Hodge & Co), H. L. Adam observed the coincidence of murder dates with Chapman's movements. The first had occurred just after Chapman had arrived in Britain, and continued during his stay when he lived in Whitechapel or nearby. Between 1891 and 1893 Ripper murders occurred in America and stopped in London. Chapman's excursion across the Atlantic coincided with this period. Chapman often posed as an American, speaking in the same style as the Americanisms in the most authentic of the Ripper letters.

However, Chapman's physical appearance was greatly at odds with all the contemporary descriptions of suspects. He was younger in 1888 (twenty-three) than any suspects mentioned, and the frequently mentioned elegant style of dress, especially that of the suspect seen by Hutchinson, also puts a query against the relatively scruffy Chapman's involvement.

H. L. Adam puts up a convincing case, and his view was initially shared by Inspector Abberline. Some years later Abberline changed his views. (See 'Pedachenko', page 137.) In the end, if Chapman is our choice, we really have to be convinced that a brutal and psychopathic sexual killer would change his spots so completely.

Score 10%

CLARENCE, HRH Prince Albert Victor, Duke of

The Clarence theory has many supporters and, like the others, has both tantalizing strengths and weaknesses.

The policeman's description of the man in Mitre Square (see page 77) could as easily have referred to Eddy as Druitt, for they bore a striking similarity to one another. Eddy could have been at the murder scenes and certainly had been found in the company of women – and men – outside the circles in which one might expect royalty to mix. Motive? it is hard to see one. But if syphilitic softening of the brain was taking place, as Dr Stowell claimed, it is possible, though medically unlikely, that this could have resulted in the sick violence exhibited by the Ripper.

Frank Spiering's claim that the Duke's death in 1892 resulted from a morphine overdose arranged by the Palace and administered by a royal physician, is uncomfortably close to the revelations in the *Sun* (27 November 1986) that the death of Eddy's brother King George V in 1936 had been similarly hastened (for different reasons) by the royal physician. This was a claim that the Palace did not deny.

Although appealing, the interesting and dramatic theory that places the Ripper high in the land has its drawbacks.

The Court Circular indicates that Eddy was in Scotland the day after Eddowes' murder, but she was killed early on Sunday morning, allowing time enough to let the train take the strain. Similar alibis, such as attending his father's birthday celebration at Sandringham, place Eddy away from the crimes, but in each case not impossibly far away. (For example Kelly had been murdered the day before the Sandringham celebration.)

Perhaps the weakest part of Stowell's theory is the evidence of the Duke's itinerary (see page 101). If Eddy was the Ripper, then we have to believe that the Royal Family, distraught at the Kelly killing, committed Eddy to an asylum, only to release him six months later to open a dock in Belfast.

It is perplexing to consider the curious caveat in the will of Eddy's father, King Edward VII. He instructed that all his (the King's) private

George Chapman. The evidence that linked the Polish barber-surgeon to the Whitechapel crimes was purely circumstantial. What convinced Inspector Abberline that the triple wife-poisoner could also be the sadistic Ripper?

papers should be destroyed. Any history book will tell us why 'Bertie', having enjoyed a very full life, might prefer his secrets to die with him. But he left similar instructions regarding his Queen's papers, and she could have had no such reasons for confidentiality. What was their secret?

There is one final strand to the Clarence theory – Stowell's claim that the Prince had not died of 'flu at Sandringham, but of softening of the brain in a mental home. Would the Royal Family really commit one of its members to an asylum, and then publicly proclaim his death, while in fact he was still alive and incarcerated? Surely this is the most preposterous hypothesis of all?

Perhaps not. Startling revelations about events in our own time suggest that perhaps Stowell's theory is not quite as incredible as it at first seems. On Monday, 6 April 1987 a *Today* newspaper article proclaimed:

> Queen's dead cousin alive.
> Palace stays silent over cover-up claim.
>
> Buckingham Palace last night refused to comment on a report that a supposedly dead cousin of the Queen had been living in a mental home for forty years.

The newspaper was reporting on an exclusive story in the *Sun*, whose headline 'Queen's cousin locked in madhouse', preceded a three-page disclosure about Katherine Bowes-Lyon, who was alleged to have spent most of her life in Royal Earlswood Mental Hospital, Redhill, Surrey.

The report, among such sub-headings as 'Written-off as dead' and 'Scandal of the Cousins the Royals forgot,' claimed that Katherine (sixty) and her elder sister Nerissa, daughters of the Queen Mother's brother, had been genetically handicapped and had been inmates at the dilapidated state-run mental hospital since 1941. Nerissa had died in January 1986 and was buried in a pauper's grave in Redhill cemetery.

The *Sun* published her death certificate, dated 22 January 1986. Above it was an extract from *Burke's Peerage* which listed Nerissa's death as having taken place in 1940 and Katherine's in 1961. Entries in that ancestral 'bible' of members of the nobility have to be approved by the head of the family before publication.

Sir Brian Rix, Secretary-General of MENCAP (The Royal Society for Mentally Handicapped Children and Adults), speaking compassionately about the Royal Family, is quoted as saying; 'Things like this did happen in families. It was an old Victorian concept: out of sight, out of mind.'

Could it be that the old Victorian concept was used in the case of Eddy, and that he was indeed out of mind, and therefore best kept out of sight?

Score 60%

Sir William Gull, John Netley and another

One of the principal snags in this ingenious tale is the question mark over the detail of four women who were killed apparently without reason. Mary Kelly, as the alleged blackmailer, had to be killed – that can be understood – but four others? Why? Hardly because they knew too much, who would have believed them? Sickert Jr claimed that the killings took place in order that nobody would notice the final murder and so link it with the Royal Family. A highly improbable, if enthralling story.

If these suspects were your choice and if Walter Sickert was the third man, then you will see in many of his paintings symbols of the victims and their wounds.

Likewise, if you selected these men as the culprits, you have to believe that senior members of the government, sober men of sound judgment, allowed the membership of a brotherhood to push them to stop at nothing to achieve their personal and political ends. Governments don't work like that. Do they?

Score 40%

The Lodgers

So little is known about these candidates that it is difficult to pay more than passing attention to them. However, if your choice is the mysterious student-lodger, you are walking with the great creative Ripperologists, those who have crafted films, plays and stories around this shadowy figure.

Score 10%

GULL, Sir William (alternative theory)

The idea of the lone doctor, stalking the streets of Whitechapel, is scarcely worth considering. Could a man of seventy possibly have had not only the strength necessary to commit the murder but also the agility to get away? He matches no descriptions of suspects at the scene. Could he have escaped in a hansom cab perhaps? Would such transport have gone unnoticed in the early hours in those mean streets?

If, as was claimed, Gull was seen in Whitechapel, could it have been for the purpose of catching and certifying one of his patients? Stowell thought so. The relaxation of police vigilance after Mary Kelly's death could be explained by the knowledge that the perpetrator was now restrained in a mental home. It could also explain why the Coroner deliberately chose to suppress evidence. But this clue could as easily be applied to the Duke of Clarence.

If Gull had been certified insane, why the necessity for a bogus funeral? The public were crying out for reassurance, and it is virtually certain that the police would have made their capture public. An unlikely suspect.

Score 10%

STEPHEN, James Kenneth

The Ripper trails frequently seem to end with the charred remnants of documents destroyed by a grieving family. That of Stephen is no exception. Who was Gull's 'S'? It may have been Stephen. He certainly exhibited signs of hatred of women and sadistic violence. The question still remains, why Whitechapel?

One point in this theory's favour is that Stephen's handwriting bears some similarity to that in the Ripper letters, but then again there is yet another theory that he sent them to cover-up Eddy's activities! In any case, the theory which suspects Stephen is based not on five murders, but on ten – all committed on royal anniversaries – and each murder claim stretches credulity more and more. In the absence of more evidence – unlikely to be turned up now that the documents have been destroyed – we would do well to concentrate on more obvious suspects.

Score 10%

Jill the Ripper/Butcher – Slaughterer/Bill the Ripper

It is difficult not to suspect that some uniformed person who could move freely, and if caught have a reasonable explanation for a bloodstained appearance near the body, might be responsible for the terrible crimes. (Even the bloodstained apron of the *shochet* was a familiar 'uniform'.)

A nurse, alone or accompanied, is a possibility. An abattoir slaughterer or butcher, like a nurse, would have a degree of skill with a knife, but a motive is not easily identifiable – though madness may be its own motivator. Police were looking for a slaughterman very early on in the crimes, and it would be reasonable to suppose that such a man might have been frightened away to another area, rather than staying in his own neighbourhood.

Policeman Ripper is a difficult theory to test, but cannot be discounted too readily. The earliest murders caused large numbers of strangers in police uniform to be drafted in to the area, and the later presence of a rogue policeman – bogus or otherwise – must be considered.

Score 10%

Dr Stanley

The revenge quest of a broken-hearted father is an appealing theory, but author Leonard Matters leaves too many questions unanswered. Would the surgeon really have killed four others before Kelly? Subject to medical knowledge at that time, according to the pathologist Kelly did not appear to have syphilis.

Kelly's popularity in an area where she had lived for a couple of years makes it unlikely that the diligent searcher would have taken some months to find her. In any case, Dr Stanley is not listed in the 1888 register of the General Medical Council of Great Britain.

These considerations would seem to rule out the mysterious Dr Stanley, who has never been traced.

Score 0%

Dr Merchant

This theory, one of the newest, also seems one of the least likely. The mere presence of a respectably dressed man talking to prostitutes lends itself to too many interpretations. Doctor Merchant seemed to be in no rush to do anything more than talk to the women, behaving in much the same way as any of the many respectably dressed philanthropists and social reformers in the East End at that time. His refusal to answer PC Spicer's questions may, in the prevailing circumstances, have been unfortunate, but it was his right to refuse.

Ten inspectors who interviewed Merchant at the police station soon formed the view that he was innocent, and there is really nothing in the Dr Merchant theory today, despite diligent and painstaking research by Brian Reilly, that can allow us to do anything other than share their view. If only they'd opened his bag. ...

Score 10%

Pedachenko/Ostrog/Konovalov

Thriller-writer William Le Queux claimed to have unearthed this theory from the papers of Rasputin. (*Things I Know*: 1923.) Donald McCormick's theory is an extension of this. According to the manuscript, Nideroest, the secret police spy, had revealed Pedachonko as the perpetrator of the Whitechapel crimes. In reviewing the first publication of the details, the *Star* poured scorn on the claim, and ridiculed the originator, Nideroest, as a charlatan who made a dubious and sparse living out of concocting half-truths against the British government.

An interesting comment on the Le Queux theory was found in graphologist Dr Dutton's *Chronicles of Crime* (unpublished). Le Queux had stated that Pedachenko was a doctor at a Russian hospital. Dutton added to this a discovery of his own. Pedachenko, he said, was Klosowski's (Chapman) double. He based this on the fact that Pedachenko had worked as a barber-surgeon for a hairdresser named Delahaye in Westmoreland Road, Walworth, south London. A check in the Post Office directory confirms the existence of the hairdresser at that address.

It was this piece of information that convinced Inspector Abberline that he was mistaken in thinking that Klosowski (Chapman) was the Ripper. Klosowski, the Polish barber-surgeon, had a double: Pedachenko, the Russian barber-surgeon. The man seen in George Yard, Spitalfields, with the murder victim Martha Tabram was not Klosowski, but Pedachenko.

Macnaghten, in his notes, mentioned Ostrog (Pedachenko) as one of his suspects:

> ... Michael Ostrog, a Russian doctor, and a convict, who was subsequently detained in a lunatic asylum as a homicidal maniac. This man's antecedents were of the worst possible type, and his whereabouts at the time of the murder could never be ascertained.

It is a tortuous track in the Ripper trail, and why the Russian barber-surgeon posed as Klosowski has never been explained. Not least of the problems in accepting this theory is that Dr Dutton's unpublished manuscript disappeared after he died in 1935, and consequently, the facts are unverified.

If Pedachenko is your choice you are in good company. Chief Inspector Abberline, Sir Melville Macnaghten and the splendid story-teller Donald McCormick all share it. You should at least get a shot at the Agatha Christie prize for welcoming complicated plots!

Score 40%

Dr Neill Cream

Will the real Dr Cream stand up please? Was there a double committing the Whitechapel murders while Cream was in an American prison? It's possible. But to allow it we have to be content that at the moment of his execution, Cream was actually thinking of repaying favours.

Score 5%

DEEMING, Frederick Bailey

Deeming's claim to be Jack the Ripper is an odd one – the crimes of which he stood accused of were in themselves bad enough: why should he wish to be held responsible for a series of even more terrible murders? It is hard to know why he made this claim. He was in prison at the time of the Whitechapel crimes.

Score 0%

PIZER, Jack (John)

Jack Pizer seems to have been treated badly enough in print during his lifetime let alone now, if that unflattering description of him by the ungenerous reporter for the *East London Observer* is anything to go by. Could such a man really have moved stealthily around the night-time streets unnoticed?

If this suspect is your choice then Sir Robert Anderson is smiling down on you. And the shade of Jack Pizer isn't.

Score 10%

MILES, Frank

This theory deserves a prize for artistic merit. Few believe it. The discrepancy between Miles' published and actual death is puzzling, but hardly enough to lay the crimes at his door. I don't think he did it, but I'll be delighted if you read the entire works of Oscar Wilde, find the clues, and prove me wrong.

Score 5%

Assorted bon-bons

There are yet more choices of suspects, some of them reasonably viable. The list is seemingly endless.

William Booth, founder of the Salvation Army, had a male secretary who predicted the murders in his dreams. Following one murder he vanished, leaving Booth convinced that the man was the Ripper.

Aleister Crowley, flamboyant occultist, wrote that the highly-respected founder of the Theosophical Society, one Madame Blavatsky, was the Ripper, and at least one biographer has taken him seriously. Crowley's prose was ambiguous and it is very unlikely that he was serious in his suggestion that the extremely overweight lady was stalking victims in the East End. What he did believe was that the mysterious killer was a hard-drinking astrologer and occultist named Dr Donstan, who was in search of supreme magical power.

Magic was part of another theory, sent to *The Times* by their Vienna correspondent. *Diebslichter* or 'thieves' candles' were useful to thieves

John Morrison, ever-purposeful in his pursuit of justice for Mary Kelly. Was there a Broadmoor cover up?

because, according to superstition, their light induced hypnotic trance. The candles were made from the uterus and other female organs. The practice of manufacturing them was still current in 1875.

A stone's throw from St Patrick's cemetery, Leyton, lives John Morrison, who feels so strongly about the final Ripper murder that he has had a memorial stone erected to Mary Kelly.

Morrison claims that Mary was killed by her common-law husband James Kelly, a convicted wife murderer who had escaped from Broadmoor criminal lunatic asylum. Kelly murdered his wife for the sake of his pregnant lover, Mary, but she deserted him during his trial and fled to London from Liverpool in fear. After his escape from Broadmoor Kelly went in search of her to exact his terrible revenge. Any prostitute questioned in his search was murdered to cover his tracks. Morrison claims that after Mary's murder, his mission completed, James Kelly – alias Jack the Ripper – stopped killing.

For the next forty years Kelly travelled the world, from France to America and finally back to England, where he is said to have been accused of the robbery of a large sum in gold, stolen at the time of his escape. He denied the charge and asked to be re-admitted to Broadmoor. The authorities refused on the grounds that he had successfully remained at large for so long. They insisted that he would be charged with robbery. It was then that Kelly claimed to be the Whitechapel killer of forty-one years before and was subsequently re-admitted to the asylum. He died in 1929. Mystery surrounds his re-admission – Broadmoor files remain closed and the authorities refuse to offer useful comment.

John Morrison, in his search for justice for Mary Kelly, maintains that Scotland Yard has covered up the identity of her killer for almost a century. He has caused questions to be directed to the Prime Minister and the House of Lords and is determined that the James Kelly Broadmoor file should be made public.

For many years successive editions of the *Guiness Book of Records* told of the escape of James Kelly, recounting his successful attempt on 28 January 1888, using a pass key made from a corset spring. He remained at large for thirty-nine years and lived in New York and Paris, eventually seeking re-admission to Broadmoor in April 1927. The record book tells how this was arranged after some difficulties, and records his death shortly afterwards.

When an MP asked questions about details of inmate James Kelly, the entry ' Longest escape from Broadmoor' ceased to appear, despite the fact that the feat had not been superseded. The mystery is heightened by the record book publisher's announcement that the reference will not be included in future editions, combined with a determination not to be quoted.

James Kelly, Whitechapel murderer, true or false? Until the papers are made public, and that could be well into the next century, we cannot know.

A theory that the Ripper might have been a 'wronged husband' is an interesting twist in the trail. Deserted by a harlot wife, he and his children could only wait beside the fireside wondering why she had left them. A medical man, he would have access to the files from prostitute's clinics. A doctor whose wife had turned whore. But would he wreak such a terrible revenge?

Sir Arthur Conan Doyle was convinced that the Ripper was female – a berserk midwife. His first Sherlock Holmes story *A Study in Scarlet* (Ward Lock, 1888) appeared in the year of the Whitechapel murders, and the great detective writer acknowledged inspiration from the crimes.

The tables were turned some years ago when another theory, hardly tenable, was published. The writer claimed that Sir Arthur himself was the Ripper.

So our parade of suspects is ended. Our spinning zoetrope has slowed for a moment to allow us to observe, and point the finger of suspicion. Some images are shadowy and private, others well-known public figures of their time. Some stand suspect because of other crimes proven against them. A few are condemned from their own utterances. Others stand out because of their lifestyles, which were thought of then – and perhaps now – as odd. Some living out lives as solo, unremarkable, even sad figures, others with the weight of power, authority and influential society behind them.

The facts about Jack the Ripper are sparse. All the evidence is circumstantial. As we have seen, successive commentators have expounded numerous pet theories, each disagreeing with the other.

Time has eventually done what the authorities never could. It has caught up with Jack and, whoever he was he has moved on, leaving us still to puzzle and ponder. The parade has passed by and now only the shadows remain.

Bibliography

Adam, H. L., *The Trial of George Chapman* (Wm Hodge & Co, 1930)

Anderson, Sir Robert, *The Lighter Side of My Official Life* (Hodder & Stoughton, 1910 & 1948)

Farson, Daniel, *Jack the Ripper* (Michael Joseph, 1972)

Fido, Martin, *Oscar Wilde* (Hamlyn, 1973; Cardinal, 1976)

Harrison, Michael, *Clarence* (W. H. Allen, 1972)

Honeycombe, Gordon, *Murders of the Black Museum* (Hutchinson, 1982)

Knight, Stephen, *Jack the Ripper—The Final Solution* (George G. Harrap, 1976; Grafton 1986)

LeQueux, William, *Things I Know about Kings, Celebrities and Crooks* (Eveleigh, Nash & Grayson, 1923)

Longford, Elizabeth, *Victoria RI* (Weidenfeld & Nicolson, 1964)

Macnaghten, Sir Melville, *Days of My Years* (Edward Arnold, 1915)

Marjoribanks, Edward, *The Life of Sir Edward Marshall Hall* (Victor Gollancz, 1929)

Matters, Leonard, *The Mystery of Jack the Ripper* (Hutchinson, 1929; W. H. Allen, 1949)

McCormick, Donald, *The Identity of Jack the Ripper* (Jarrolds, 1959; Pan, 1962; Arrow & J. Long, 1970)

McWhirter, Norris (ed.), *The Guinness Book of Records* (Guinness Superlatives, 1975)

Pope-Hennessy, James, *Queen Mary* (George Allen & Unwin, 1959)

Quennell, Peter (ed.), *Mayhew's London Underworld* (Century Hutchinson, 1987)

Rumbelow, Donald, *The Complete Jack the Ripper* (W. H. Allen, 1975)

Wilks, S., and Bettany, G. T., *Biographical History of Guy's Hospital* (Ward Lock, 1892)

Williams, Watkin W., *The Life of General Sir Charles Warren* (Blackwell, 1941)

Wilson, Colin, *A Criminal History of Mankind* (Granada, 1984; Grafton Books, 1985)

Wilson, Colin and Pitman, Patricia, *Encyclopaedia of Murder* (Arthur Barker, 1961)

Index

Abberline, Inspector 80, 82, 96, 98, 129, 136
Adam, H. L. 129
Alexandra, Princess of Wales 102, 103
Anderson, Sir Robert 53, 106, 108, 126, 138
Arnold, Supt. 45, 80, 83

Backert, Albert 95–6, 128
Baderski, Lucy 97, 98
Barnardo, Dr Thomas John 42
Barnett, Joseph ('husband' of Mary Kelly) 59, 79
Bagster-Phillips, Dr George 26–8, 30, 79, 84
Baxter, Dr Wynne 30, 77
Bedford, Revd R. C. 67–9
Berner St 37–42, 77
Blavatsky, Mme 138
bloodhounds 54, 80
Booth, William 138
Bowyer, Thomas 62–3
Brough, Edward 54, 80
Buck's Row 16–21, 77
Butler, Arthur 113

Chapman, Annie (victim No 2) 26–32, 77, 104, 126
Chapman, George (Severin Antoniovich Klosowski) 96, 127, 129, 136–7
Clarence, HRH Prince Albert Victor, Duke of 98–106, 111, 131–3
Coles, Francis 86, 121
Conan Doyle, Sir Arthur 113, 141
Contagious Diseases Act (1864) 23
Conway, Thomas 46
Cox, Mary Ann 77, 85
Cream, Dr Thomas Neill 120–2, 137
Crook, Annie Elizabeth 103–4
Crowley, Aleister 138
Cummins, Gordon 87–8
Cutbush, Thomas 86

Daily Telegraph, the 36, 67, 77, 79, 84
Davis, John 26
Dearden, Dr Harold 102
Deeming, Frederick Bailey 122–3, 137
De Salvo, Alberto 90
Diemshitz, Lewis 37–8, 40–2
Donovan, Timothy 28, 30
Dorset Street 44, 57, 82
Druitt, Montague John 92–6, 128

Dutton, Dr Thomas 73, 136

Eddowes, Catherine (victim No 4) 43–9, 78, 131

Farson, Dan 129
fingerprints 73–5
Flower & Dean Street 42, 47, 56
Forbes-Winslow, Dr A. 67, 109, 112
freemasonry 51–3, 103, 106, 107–8

Garrett, Pulteney 33
Glasgow 35, 73
Gordon Brown, Dr Frederick 47–8
Gull, Sir William 99–100, 102, 103–8, 109–10, 111, 133, 134
Gutteridge, PC 84

Haine, PC 18
Hanbury Street 26–7, 77, 126
Harrison, Michael 102, 111–12
Harvey, Maria 59
Heath, Neville 88
Herd, Richard 113–14
Hitchcock, Alfred 109
Holland, Emily 18–19
Hutchinson (witness to Mary Kelly murder) 60–2, 78

Illustrated Police News 17, 29, 34–5, 67, 76, 79, 112

Jack the Ripper: anatomical expertise 94, 115–16, 135; handwriting 68, 73; letters from 48, 64–8, 71–5; possible appearance 32, 42, 49, 60, 77–8, 85, 91; pranksters 33–6, 66; subsequent similar crimes 87–90; suspects 92f; a woman? 112–14, 135
Jack the Ripper, studies of: Clarence (Harrison) 102, 111–12; The Complete Jack the Ripper (Rumbelow) 117; The Identity of Jack the Ripper (McCormick) 65, 119–20; Jack the Ripper, The Final Solution (Knight) 106–8; The Mystery of Jack the Ripper (Matters) 118, 135; Prince Jack (Spiering) 100; The Trial of George Chapman (Adam) 129
Jackson, Elizabeth 86
Jago, Fred W. P. 73–5

Jewish community 45, 108, 114–16, 124

Kelly, James ('husband' of Mary
  Kelly) 140–1
Kelly, John ('husband' of Catherine
  Eddowes) 47
Kelly, Mary Jeanette (victim No 5) 10–12,
  57–63, 76, 78–85, 104, 110, 135, 140–1
Kent, Constance 112
Kiss, Bela 87
Klosowski, Severin Antoniovich *see* Chapman,
  George
Knight, Stephen 106–8
Kurten, Peter 87

Le Queux, William 136
'Leather Apron' *see* Pizer, John
Lees, Robert 109–10
Lewis, Sarah 82
Liverpool 72
Llewellyn, Dr 20
Long, PC Alfred 44–5
Lusk, George 48

McCarthy, John 57, 62–3
McCormick, Donald 65, 119–20, 136–7
McDonald, Dr Roderick 77, 78–9, 84
MacKenzie, Alice 86
Macnaghten, Sir Melville 54, 83, 96, 120,
  128, 137
Marshall, William 42
Marshall Hall, Sir Edward 122, 123
Matters, Leonard 118, 135
Matthews, Henry, Home Secretary 53,
  54–5, 70–1, 84
Maxwell, Caroline 82
Merchant, Dr 118, 136
Metropolitan Police Act (1839) 22
Miles, Frank 127, 138
Miller's Court 57–65, 77, 79–83, 110
Mitre Square 43–6, 77
Morris, George 43–4

Netley, John 103, 104, 105, 108, 133
newspaper reports and comment 17, 20, 29,
  30, 34–5, 36, 67, 70, 107
newspapers, letters to 67–9, 73–5
Nichols, Mary ('Polly' victim No 1) 16–21,
  25, 70, 77, 104, 124, 125
Nichols, William 18, 20

Ostrog, Mikhail, *see* Pedachenko, Dr

Payne, Cynthia 24
Pedachenko, Dr (Mikhail Ostrog) 119–20,
  136–7
photography, forensic 83
Pizer, John ('Leather Apron') 25, 123–7,
  138

practical jokes 33–6
Prater, Elizabeth 82
Princess Alice (steamer) 39–40
prostitution and the law 22–4

Rasputin 119, 136
Ratcliffe Highway 15, 79
Reilly, Brian 118, 136
rewards 70–1
Rogers, Revd William 69
Rumbelow, Donald 57, 93, 117

Salisbury, Lord, Prime Minister 53, 104
Shaw, George Bernard 69–70
Sickert, Joseph 103–7, 133
Sickert, Walter 103–8, 128, 133
Skoptsi sect 116
Smith, Emma 25, 86, 97
Smith, Maj. Henry 44, 45, 48
Smith, PC William 39, 42
Spicer, Robert 118, 136
Spiering, Frank 100, 131
Spinks, Mary 97
spiritualism 109–10
Staniak, Lucien 88–90
Stanley, Dr 118, 135
Star, The 20, 35, 36, 54, 69
Stephen, James Kenneth 110–12, 134
Stowell, Dr Thomas 98–102, 110, 111, 131,
  134
Stride, Elizabeth ('Long Liz', victim
  No 3) 39–42, 49, 77, 104
Stride, John Thomas 39–40
Sun, the 113, 131, 132
Sutcliffe, Peter ('Yorkshire Ripper') 90

Tabram, Martha 25, 56, 86, 109, 137
Thrawl Street 18, 56
Times, The 30, 54, 64, 70, 72, 114–15
Toughill, Thomas 127

Vacher, Joseph 87
Vagrancy Act (1824) 22
venereal disease 23, 100–1, 122–3
Victoria, Queen 66–7, 100–1, 109–10
Violenia, Emmanuel 126

Warren, Sir Charles 45, 50–5, 76–7, 80, 83
Watkins, PC 43
Webber, Jeanne 112
Wentworth-Bell, G. 109
Whitechapel Vigilance Committee 48, 53,
  70, 72, 95
Wilde, Oscar 127
Wilson, Colin 102

'Yorkshire Ripper' (Peter Sutcliffe) 90